Casey Anthony has received and will receive *no money* from any sales of this book.

Advance Praise

The authors go below the surface and dive into what really happened to Caylee. They write clearly from their vast experience in child advocacy, law, psychiatry, psychology, grief counseling and spirituality to give us a compelling "who-done-it" and analysis of a trial that millions have followed.

Wendy Murphy gives us a clear account from her detailed study of this trial and her conclusions about why Caylee died. Charles Whitfield shows us what child abuse and neglect are and how to prevent more such tragic deaths to innocent children like Caylee. And Barbara Whitfield applies what we know from grief counseling and near-death studies to give us ways to process our own pain over this injustice.

—Bruce Greyson MD
Carlson Professor of Psychiatry & Neurobehavioral Sciences, University of Virginia School of Medicine

A brilliant analysis—painful but open and honest. This book speaks to a reality that many of us would like to ignore because the violence and abuse that this one little girl experienced is all too common in the lives of children all over the world. Insightful and innovative.

—Gail Dines PhD
Professor of Sociology, Chair of American Studies, Wheelock College, Author, *Pornland*

i

This horrific story and trial has mesmerized and traumatized the public. This book comes to the rescue. The three authors' respective areas of expertise masterfully converge and we are gently led through the legal, psychological and spiritual perspectives that ultimately enable us to find clarity and peace. These three—all experts in their fields—shed light on utter darkness.

—Judith Miller PhD
Professor of Developmental Psychology,
Columbia University

So much information, wisdom and compassion is compressed into this timely work. Everyone can benefit from reading it.

Wendy Murphy JD dissects with precision the failings of the legal process and passionately advocates for all children suffering abuse.

Charles Whitfield MD brings his many years of experience and clinical wisdom to bear on this case and shows the reader how to understand the inter-generational dynamics of child abuse and the ways to prevent it and heal from it.

Barbara Whitfield RT adds her decades of clinical, research and personal experience to show the reader the importance of facing the hurts and losses to be grieved.

—Lawrence Edwards PhD
Faculty, New York Medical College,
Department of Family Medicine
Author, *The Soul's Journey*

If you were angry or disappointed by the verdict, this is a must-read for anyone who believes in justice for children. Wendy Murphy's riveting analysis of the case reveals facts and evidence that jurors and the public never heard. Her courageous work to uncover the truth about Caylee's death is crucial: too often children die behind closed doors and without a voice. Charles and Barbara Whitfield offer their wisdom and experience as to what we can do better on behalf of all children and as well as extraordinary insights about what we can do right now to find meaning in the death of Caylee Anthony.

—Eileen King
Regional Director, Justice for Children DC

A fascinating account of real life mystery and intrigue as viewed though a scientific lens by a team of true professionals. Wendy Murphy takes complex information and presents it in an easy-to-understand and compelling manner. Dr. Whitfield explores child abuse and its many components, and offers a unique approach to healing, recovery and prevention. Barbara Whitfield's contribution is clear and invaluable.

—Clancy D McKenzie MD
Author, *Babies Need Mothers*

On The Cover

Caylee Anthony's life was caught between strong forces—some adults who abused, neglected, ignored and finally killed her. Instead of looking after her welfare, *they looked away*.

Caylee's death was obscured by people who cared only for themselves. They looked toward money, parties, lies, false claims, video stores, cars, and their own personal survival. Day after day seemingly clever ineptitude in and out of the courtroom buried Caylee again under reams of paper that contain mostly meaningless words. Everyone was *looking away*.

Those who were entrusted with finding truth and administering Justice looked blindly away. Sometimes they appeared self-satisfied as *they looked away*.

But Caylee didn't know how to look away. She looked hopefully and expectantly toward her mother and others for love, but they looked away.

An enraged community and nation *did not* look away.

These pictures on the cover are metaphors meant to illustrate the way responsible adults looked away from a child in need.

May we learn from Caylee's death to look often to the needs of every child, everywhere, and at all times.

May we never look away again —db

CASEY ANTHONY

What REALLY Happened to Caylee?

— and Why Truth Matters

THE EVIDENCE THEY DIDN'T TELL YOU

WHAT CASEY AND HER LAWYERS
DON'T WANT YOU TO KNOW

AND

THE TRUTH ABOUT WHY CAYLEE DIED

WITH STRATEGIES FOR HOW TO PREVENT
CHILD ABUSE AND NEGLECT DEATHS

Wendy Murphy JD

with

Charles L. Whitfield MD
and
Barbara H. Whitfield RT

ꟿ𝕳P
muse house press

ꟿꞖP
muse house press

ISBN: 978-1-935827-08-5

Trade Paperback
© Copyright 2011 Wendy Murphy, Charles Whitfield,
and Barbara Whitfield

Request for information and rights should be
addressed to:
    Muse House Press

Find us on the Internet at:
    www.MuseHousePress.com

Muse House Press and the Muse House Press logo are
imprints of Muse House Press, Inc.

Find Wendy on the Internet at:
    PatriotLedger.com/opinions/opinions_columnists

Find Charles and Barbara on the Internet at:
    www.Barbara-Whitfield.Blogspot.com

Cover Design: Donald Brennan
Interior Composition: Donald Brennan

"Blind Justice" painting by Kinuko Y. Craft.

Printed in the United States of America
First Printing, Galley

Statement of Intention

In this book we are presenting our observations and opinions from a legal, clinical, medical and psychological perspective. The opinions expressed in this book are of the three authors individually and reflect what we as experts in our own fields know about childhood trauma, abuse and neglect.

All information quoted in this book has already been presented publicly throughout the media or in the public transcripts. This is all in the public record. We have organized and summarized what we see as the essential events and dynamics before and during the trial and raise key issues and questions that have not been addressed elsewhere. We see the cause of this tragedy as a systemic malfunction (page 197), and we blame no one individual. Healing begins with accurately naming what happened, not blaming.

Dedication

We dedicate this book to the millions of children who have been and are being abused and neglected in this country and the world. This includes the five children who *die* from abuse and neglect daily in this country.

We dedicate this book to trauma survivors of all ages who can identify with any of the people involved in this tragic story.

We dedicate this book to all attorneys, advocates and clinicians who work to assist these trauma survivors.

Most of all, we dedicate this book to you, the reader, in the hope that you believe, as we do, that truth matters.

Acknowledgments

Thanks to all the passionate people in Florida and beyond who stood in front of the courthouse and the Anthony home protesting the cruelty done to one little girl.

You made us take notice, stop our usual lives and listen to the hidden secret that plagues our humanity—child abuse and neglect.

Thank you to Caylee Marie Anthony, an innocent child who came into this lifetime with all the potential and hope that each of us brings. Hopefully, your tragic role in this story is shining a light that will illuminate the darkness for all children.

We also thank the countless reporters and bloggers who kept the spotlight on this story so that we couldn't escape its tragic lesson.

Thank you to Ram Dass for allowing us to reproduce the letter to grievers. You can find the original letter in *The Natural Soul* and on line at *www.ramdasstapes.org/articles_final.htm*

As painful as this story is, there is still hope that it will inspire us to examine our abusive and neglectful attitude toward children, and to work harder to respect and protect their needs and their rights as human beings.

—WM, CLW, BHW

Table of Contents

Contents   Page

Part One: Legal Aspects

The Investigation, Pretrial Proceedings,

Trial and Post-Trial

by Wendy Murphy JD

Exhibits

Foreword

by Charles L. Whitfield MD

This trial, in its essence, reveals a common truth about repeated childhood trauma and its detrimental effects on the lives of our children and on society as a whole: Childhood trauma is inter- and trans-generational. As was said a long time ago, "The sins of the fathers shall be visited upon the sons and daughters." Unstopped, the abuse and neglect of children becomes a vicious cycle that produces victims who tend to grow up to become abusers themselves.

By exposing some of the underlying facts and reasons behind the murder of one little girl, we hope to make the world safer for all children.

At a minimum, we hope this book will unveil more of the essential truth in this perplexing drama. Wendy Murphy's background as a fierce advocate for children and experienced legal analyst who has covered high profile trials for many networks over the past fifteen years provides a compelling perspective of the evidence we've seen, and a lot we haven't seen. Much of what seems significant was never admitted as evidence at trial. Our primary concern is that this trial was not about the truth. Too much of the case remains under seal.

The Contents of This Book

Wendy explains in the first ten chapters why *what we didn't hear* during trial may well matter more than what was revealed in the courtroom. Each chapter is followed by photographs of transcripts or evidence that was not introduced at trial, but that bears significantly on the underlying truth.

In the remaining chapters, my wife and I write about the nature of trauma, not only in the life of an abused or neglected child but also in the lives of so many of us who watched this case unfold and felt hurt by the story, as well as by the verdict.

To make this book more useful, we have included in the **Appendix** a new and expanded **Timeline** of key events in this case, many of which have not been published elsewhere. We also include an educational graphic, *Casey's Complex and Tangled Web*, that depicts key players and dynamics.

Finally, we finish with a chapter on possible future events and dynamics for Casey as she navigates her way back into society, and for all of us, as we wrestle with feelings of anger, frustration and concern for a little girl who died a horrible death.

Our Strong Reaction

The public's strong reaction to this case, fueled to a large extent by anger toward Casey and compassion for Caylee, reflects our concern and outrage that any parent could fail to report a vulnerable child missing for 31 days. Like most childhood trauma that goes unnoticed, we see this aspect of the case as proof that something is wrong not only with our *legal system*, but also with our *morality* and even our *news media*—that a child's life could be so unimportant, a toddler could be missing for a whole month before anyone takes serious steps to find her. If this case is an indication of how little value we place on children's lives, imagine all the other forms of abuse and neglect that must be going on with kids—harm that doesn't rise to the level of murder, about which we know nothing because so much of child abuse happens behind closed doors.

An estimated 70 to 80% of us grew up with some degree of childhood trauma from dysfunctional families. The detrimental and painful effects of family dysfunction permeate our adult lives unless and until we take steps to understand the nature of the harm, and begin to heal through safe and non-toxic treatment and recovery.

Nearly all trauma survivors have feelings of empathy and compassion for people who have endured similarly difficult experiences. People with antisocial personality disorder (ASPD), whether or not they suffered trauma as a child, lack such capacity for empathy. Yet we know that underneath most personality disorders and mental illnesses lie toxic familial and sociological factors that are causally related to the perpetration of child abuse and neglect. If Casey had a personality disorder or "mental illness," it would be important to ascertain whether she suffered abuse and neglect as a child. She was a high school dropout and a single mom who was barely out of childhood herself when she assumed the extraordinary responsibility of raising a child of her own.

Was Casey the type of person to neglect a child? It's hard to say she wasn't, given that lots of healthy adults in what may appear to be ideal circumstances have the capacity to harm their own children, and others, for whom they feel sincere love. We don't know enough about Casey's background to say for sure, though people who watched the case unfold, even if they lacked medical or mental health credentials to opine, felt no compunction about declaring Casey psychologically predisposed to abuse her own child.

For example, attorney Bernie Grimm on the Fox News program *On the Record* (July 12, 2011) called Casey "morally bankrupt."

It's not clear whether the jury agreed with Grimm. And if they did, it's a testament to our legal system that a jury can judge the facts objectively without relying on strong emotions to decide the case. One juror reported after the verdict that the first vote they took was 10 to 2 for acquittal of first-degree murder. They said they needed more evidence. A jury overwrought with emotion would have ignored the weaknesses in the state's proof and voted to convict simply because any parent who can disregard their child's absence for an entire month is probably capable of murder.

But is this logical observation the same as evidence? The jury heard about duct tape, and no doubt understood as we all do that there is no "innocent" reason to tape a child's mouth shut. But where was the proof of who put the duct tape on Caylee's body? When? Why? The jury didn't buy the prosecution's theory that Casey taped her child's mouth and nose shut so she could be free to party, and it's fair to say there are a lot of options, short of murder, for mothers who feel trapped by parenthood, as I describe in chapter 13.

Abuse and Neglect by a Mother?

For some people, the very idea that a mother could be so cruel is impossible to fathom. Even if we can accept this on some level, it's so painful to believe this idea, there's almost a built-in potential for reasonable doubt anytime a child dies an especially brutal death at the hands of their mother. We may not feel the same kind of bias toward dads, which isn't fair toward either gender, nor is it fair to the kids who desperately need to be believed when they report abuse.

It's true that mothers are less likely to kill their children than are fathers, which stands to reason from a biological point of view. The experience of giving birth produces in the mother the sense that the child is part of her. Mothers are less likely to kill their children because, in a way, it's like killing a part of themselves. The connection is less strong for fathers. This doesn't begin to explain all the differences between mothers and fathers, but it's an important concept to remember because it helps explain why we are so uncomfortable with our feelings when we hear about mothers who kill. It would behoove us all to understand our discomfort in this regard.

No child is safe so long as we romanticize motherhood to the extent we can't accept the idea that some mothers are capable of neglecting, abusing and even killing the very children they purport to love.

That said, there are many reasons to doubt Casey's *direct* involvement *in the murder* of her daughter, though there *are* good reasons to suspect her involvement in activities that were otherwise abusive and neglectful. Unfortunately, in this shocking story, the personal, social and *parenting behavior* of the mother on trial was *never fully explored* and *exposed*. We heard about some of

Casey Anthony's activities in the time period before and after Caylee went missing, but a lot of information never came out. Whether this is because there was no other evidence that Caylee was neglected or abused, or, as Wendy Murphy notes, because evidence of other harmful things that were going on in Caylee's life was excluded from trial when the court put certain information "under seal," is hard to know with certainty.

This book will attempt to shed light on some of that information in the hope of inspiring all of us to work harder to see the truth about what's going on in the lives of all children.

Our single purpose is to help ensure that no child ever again suffers the horrific fate that took the life of one little girl in Florida.

Charles L. Whitfield MD,
Atlanta, GA
October 2011

Part One: Legal Aspects

By Wendy Murphy JD

The Investigation, Pretrial Proceedings, Trial and Post-Trial

1   Introduction

Dubbed the "Trial of the Century," the prosecution of 25-year-old Florida single mom Casey Marie Anthony for the murder of her toddler daughter Caylee, could more aptly be called the Trial of the Absurd. The prosecution, headed by Assistant District Attorney Jeff Ashton, paradoxically seemed almost destined to prove Anthony's innocence, while defense attorney Jose Baez couldn't manage a single reference to the evidence that best proves Casey did not kill her child.

The public gasped in shock and disbelief when Baez blamed the child's death on an accidental drowning in his opening statement, but did anyone notice how he *failed to talk* in detail about *anything* related to the days and hours around the *time Caylee went missing*?

Did anyone see it as significant that Baez immediately got us focused on a theory that could not have been *less* connected to the real evidence in the case?

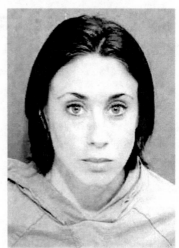

Casey's mug shot in jail

For some of us, irrespective of Baez's distraction tactics, it was clear for a long time that Casey would be found not guilty. Judging the case solely on the evidence released prior to trial, there was no doubt the prosecution's case was sorely lacking. Indeed, I wrote exactly this in an op-ed published in 2009. Here's what I said:

If lying, being a bad mother, and disposing of a dead body were enough—this case would be over. And if that's all the evidence the state has to prove its case, the defense can make reservations for its victory party right now.

It pains me to say this because when children are murdered, the "mother bear" in me comes out. And hearing about Caylee's little bones being "intermingled" with plant growth because her body was dumped like trash makes me sink my teeth into any evidence that points at guilt because, like most people, I want someone to pay for what happened to this defenseless little girl.

Aside from maternal ferocity, and the fact that as a pundit/former prosecutor I'm usually asked to argue the state's case, I tend toward the prosecution's side most of the time because studies have shown that at least 95% of people charged with a crime are guilty of something. And it matters that prosecutors are ethically obligated NOT to bring charges unless they have enough evidence to prove the case "beyond a reasonable doubt".

Nevertheless, I call 'em like I see 'em. If there's reasonable doubt, I'll say so—even if it means a dangerous criminal walks free. So if the only evidence against Casey Anthony is that which we've read about in the press, I believe she will be acquitted. The state can't possibly prove the charges without some evidence suggesting when, how, where and why Casey killed her child. So far, I've seen nothing.

A jury will surely find her repulsive and they might want desperately to punish Casey for being a wretch of a mother. But without actual evidence proving that she is legally responsible for causing her daughter's death, jurors will be obligated to vote not guilty.

In the very next sentence, I predicted a conviction notwithstanding gaping holes in the evidence because I was hopeful the state had much more proof than that which was being released during the investigation. I assumed we weren't allowed to hear about the most damning evidence in advance of trial because the judge had sealed it from public view, under one or more exceptions to Florida's public records law in order to protect Casey's fair trial rights.

Florida's Seemingly Generous "Sunshine Law"

Contrary to widespread myths about the generosity of Florida's Sunshine Law that allows for public access to information in the custody of the state, *numerous exceptions* exist that *forbid public access* to all kinds of information. For example, the law explicitly allows prosecutors to withhold information if disclosure might "jeopardize the safety of a ... witness," including the defendant, or "impair the ability of a [prosecutor] to locate or prosecute a codefendant." *Translation*: if people involved in the case had been threatened, this exception would kick in and related evidence would not be released prior to trial. Casey's mother, Cindy Anthony, told police and others that threats had been made and Lee Anthony, Casey's brother, testified at trial that Casey had been threatened not to call the cops in the days after Caylee disappeared. As early as August 10, 2008, Cindy told her brother, Rick, in an email, "there's a lot you guy's don't know" and that "the facts cannot be released for many reasons." (See Exhibit 1A). She reiterated her concerns about threats in her deposition. (See Exhibit 1B). Who made the threats? Why?

Even without evidence of threats, damning evidence against a criminal defendant can be kept secret prior to trial under another broad-sweeping exception to the Sunshine Law, adopted by the Florida Supreme Court in the *Miami Herald* case, which provides that evidence can be withheld from the public "to protect the defendant's constitutional right to a fair trial". This means that if evidence showed that Casey had been involved in prostitution, for example, the judge would have had authority to order such evidence "sealed" under the theory that Casey would not receive a fair trial if the potential jury pool, already outraged that a mother failed to report her child missing for a month, heard that she had also been involved in illegal sexual activity.

After reading the Sunshine Law carefully, I was hopeful before the trial that the case seemed weak not because there was no evidence to prove murder but because of these various exceptions to the Sunshine Law.

Two years later, I crossed my fingers when the prosecution started its opening statement, expecting the proof to be there and that Casey Anthony's guilt would be established beyond a reasonable doubt.

Re-Assessing the Evidence

I realized I was wrong as soon as the prosecution's opening statement was over. I immediately restated my opinion that the evidence was insufficient and that Casey would be acquitted. In fact, I was the first pundit to say so in writing and on television, including on NBC's Today Show. I took a lot of heat from people for having the audacity to suggest that a woman who *seemed* so guilty could, in fact, be innocent. "You're not an advocate for children," some e-mailers said. "How dare you defend such a vile person?" "Shame on you, Wendy. How can you call yourself an attorney for victims?!"

It was relentless. But as I wrote in my 2007 book *And Justice For Some*, I don't make comments to please the crowd. I take the time to read the evidence myself and I judge cases based on what I learn, rather than assuming the only information that matters is that which is reported on cable news programs. News shows don't have time to address every piece of evidence and to provide a forum for every nuanced view of information, especially in a case of this magnitude. I wanted to know as much as I could for my own purposes, so I read thousands of pages of material from the investigative file, and based on what I read, especially after hearing the prosecution's opening statement, a not guilty verdict was inevitable.

This book explains that while we may never figure out who killed little Caylee, we can solve some of the mysteries in the case by asking *and* answering important questions about the evidence. At a minimum, a full airing of more truthful information will help prevent a similar distortion of justice in the future.

To really understand what happened, we have to think about the case with a heavy emphasis on what has *not* been said, and put that absence of information together with what we *do* know. We might not end up with clarity about exactly what happened, but compared to the façade of a trial that purported to answer that question, reading this book will get us far closer to the truth.

Exhibit 1A.   Cindy's Brother Rick's email to Orange County Sheriff's Office

From: RickA1P@aol.com
Date: Thu, 21 Aug 2008 19:23:54 EDT
Subject: **Cindy's reply to my first letter.**
To: Yuri.Melich@ocfl.net

...There's alot [sic] you guys don't know and we cannot say. I can assure you I am not mad at you but the facts cannot be released for many reasons.

Exhibit 1B. Cindy Testifies about Threats

1 that I found out through Annie that that picture was

2 actually Ricardo's.

3   So I started thinking, okay, was she trying

4 to tell me Zanny's apartment --

5   Q   Is really Ricardo?

6   A   Ricardo. And I was trying to figure out the

7 connections. And we started looking in the connections

8 from Ricardo and Amy to Tony and Fusion's. And that's

9 pretty much what I went through when I was at the FBI

10 office.

11   Q   So then a month later you come to find out

12 that all this stuff that you were trying to figure out

13 through these clues and this puzzle is wrong?

14   A   Well, again, I don't know. Because to this

15 day, if Casey has been told to keep her mouth shut

16 because something would happen to Caylee or something

17 would happen to her family, which Casey said that in so

18 many words when we visited her, that I don't know if

19 she's safe, I don't know if we're safe --

20   Q   She who? Casey?

21   A   Casey. I don't know if we're safe. So when

22 Casey started telling us -- and I knew there had to be

23 a reason why she was lying so severely to me. You

24 know, I mean --

25   Q   Sure.

2 Is There Evidence that Someone *Other than Casey* Killed Caylee?

The obvious answer to this question is yes.

Cops understood from the start that *Casey knew more* than what she was saying *about why* Caylee was missing. This we know because Casey was offered immunity early on to tell what she knew about the people involved in Caylee's disappearance. (See Exhibit 2). Prosecutors don't offer immunity in a potential homicide case unless they believe the suspect has *very* valuable information to share. It's political suicide to make deals with a potential child-killer unless the prosecutor has a damn good explanation that will placate the public when they find out why he or she made a deal with the devil. The prosecution made the offer—but Casey said no. Why?

It's interesting that at the time Casey rejected an immunity deal, she was already represented by Jose Baez—an attorney Cindy said showed up out of nowhere. It's not clear who was paying him or who asked him to get involved, but Cindy told cops it wasn't her or her family. (See Exhibit 3). After the verdict, it was reported that Baez represented

Casey for a paltry sum of $90,000.00 and that he was compensated by tax dollars via a fund for indigent defendants who cannot afford a lawyer. But this fund didn't kick in until early 2010, after Baez filed a motion asking the court to declare Casey indigent. Who paid him for the first two years of preparation and representation? Some reports say he was paid with $200,000 from money ABC gave the Anthonys for a story they ran about the investigation. But Cindy was asked in her deposition about money her family had received for interviews, and she never mentioned $200,000. Did ABC give the money directly to Casey? To Baez?

In spring 2009, the prosecution ramped up the pressure on Casey when they put the death penalty on the table. If threats were made to keep her silent, as Cindy and Lee reported to cops, the death penalty leveled the playing field because she would die one way or the other. But Casey stood firm.

No doubt this is because she trusted the advice of her attorney who may have persuaded her that while the prosecution had lots of evidence that Casey lied and failed to report Caylee missing for a month, there was an excellent chance she would be acquitted because the state had no proof of who killed the child or how or when Caylee was murdered. How could the state possibly win, much less persuade the jury to vote for death?

It was a big risk given that Casey's life was on the line, but the odds were in Casey's favor because the prosecution's case left ample room for doubt.

Serious Doubts

Caylee was last seen with Casey leaving George and Cindy's home around 1 p.m. on June 16, 2008. The prosecution seemed to claim that Casey then drugged Caylee with chloroform, put her in her car trunk and taped her mouth shut sometime after 1 and before 8 p.m., though they never actually said anything about a specific date or time of death. The implication that she died on the 16th came from the fact that when Casey is seen on videotape at a Blockbuster store at around 8 p.m. with her boyfriend Tony Lazzaro, Caylee is nowhere to be seen. Though there was no actual evidence of when Caylee died, it was essentially agreed by the parties at trial that the child died on the 16th when Jose Baez declared in his opening statement, albeit with no evidence, that the child drowned on June 16th 2008.

It's certainly possible, though exceedingly unlikely, that little Caylee was already dead and in the trunk of Casey's car when Casey and Tony left Blockbuster. But the prosecution's theory was that Casey intentionally taped the child's mouth shut so she could keep Caylee quiet while she went out partying. Casey and Tony spent the night at Tony's apartment watching movies. Where was the party?

Tony Lazzaro

And if it were an accidental killing, wouldn't one piece of duct tape have been enough? As prosecutor Jeff Ashton said during the trial, the fact that three separate pieces were used to cover the nose and mouth is unassailable evidence that whoever put the tape there meant to cause the child's death, not keep her quiet for a night of partying.

The most rational view of the duct tape evidence suggests the child died before the duct tape was applied and that the tape was meant only to hold in decomposition fluids. It isn't that duct tape *couldn't* have caused Caylee's death, but there are so many more efficient ways to kill a person. It makes more sense that the tape was meant to prevent detection of the body for a time. When a dead body begins to decompose, fluids emanate from places like the nose and mouth, and they emit putrid odors. Sealing the nose and mouth delays detection.

It's certainly possible that at age 22, a high school dropout like Casey with no experience as a killer, nonetheless knew how to seal a dead body like a master murderer. And it's true that her failure to report Caylee missing for more than a month is powerful evidence of her consciousness of guilt. The question unresolved at trial was—guilt about what? Maybe Casey felt guilt about other things she was involved in, such as her own illegal activities. *If she knew* who had Caylee and had been threatened not to call the cops, as Lee said was the case, she stayed quiet because she believed she would eventually get her child back if she did not report Caylee missing. (See Exhibit 1B).

Did the Prosecution Overcharge Casey?

Since the verdict, virtually every defense attorney pundit has blamed the acquittal on the District Attorney's decision to "overcharge" the case as a death penalty prosecution. But this criticism is silly. Anyone who tapes a toddler's mouth and nose shut, whether before or after death, then wraps the body in multiple layers of bags and dumps it in a car trunk for a few days before tossing the remains in a swamp, is guilty of first degree murder. There's nothing accidental about such gruesome facts.

Is it *possible* the death was accidental, and the cover-up made to look like a more brutal crime? I suppose. Is it *possible* that Casey was the one who did this to her child? Sure. But instead of getting lost in speculation about explanations that lack common sense and sound logic, we can choose to draw reasonable inferences about more likely scenarios including that someone else could have intended the same result. Why is this a logical scenario? Because based on what we *do* know, someone other than Casey had access to the child, *and* had access to Casey's car, around the time the child went missing.

Motive, Intent and Opportunity

Solving any murder requires a focus on who had motive, intent and opportunity to kill. Let's start with opportunity. Although we know for certain that Casey had custody of Caylee until at least 1 p.m. on the 16th, there are good reasons to believe Caylee wasn't killed until June 17th, the day *after* Casey is last seen with her child.

This fact, alone, would be powerful evidence that someone else killed Caylee because we know that Casey did not have physical custody of Caylee when she was at Blockbuster at 8 p.m. on the 16th, or at anytime thereafter. Which means, whoever *did* have custody is a potential suspect.

Here's how we know Caylee probably died no sooner than June 17th:

The child's remains were found with pink and white shorts and a T-shirt bearing certain letters. The denim shorts and solid pink top she'd been wearing when she was last seen leaving George and Cindy's home on June 16th were not in the bag and apparently have never been located.

While it's possible Casey changed Caylee's entire outfit between 1 and 8 p.m., is it likely? And wouldn't the outfit from the 16th have been uncovered from Casey's car, or Tony's apartment? Why did the outfit disappear?

More on Caylee's Clothes

The bag in which Caylee's remains were found did not contain a diaper or other form of toddler undergarment. She reportedly wore "Pull-ups" at the time because she was just learning to become potty-trained. If Casey had re-dressed the child because, for example, she had a toileting accident, not only would the outfit from the 16th have shown up someplace during the investigation, the change of clothing would have likely included some kind of diaper or undergarment. Why was there no diaper or "Pull-up" in the bag with the remains?

Another oddity is that the shorts found with Caylee's remains were too small for the child. They were identified by Cindy as Caylee's, but Cindy said Caylee had long ago outgrown them and hadn't worn that particular pair of shorts since 2007. Casey left her parents' home on June 16th with a

15

bag that could have contained a change of clothes for Caylee, but would it have contained an outfit that didn't fit? Would it have failed to contain some sort of undergarment?

The remnants of the T-shirt found with Caylee's remains was *not* Caylee's. Cindy told cops Caylee never owned such a shirt and that she did not recognize the T-shirt as something Caylee had ever worn. Who would have dressed the child in a garment Cindy did not recognize? Cindy was one of Caylee's primary caregivers. She regularly bought the child new clothes, and rotated out of Caylee's wardrobe the outfits she had outgrown. Who else would have had access to the clothes found with Caylee's remains? A stranger? A deranged killer? Someone who knew Casey and Caylee?

Babysitters usually have extra clothing at their homes for the children they care for, in case they spill something, or wet their pants. Wouldn't a babysitter who had cared for Caylee likely have had custody of some of the child's clothes? Cindy testified in her deposition that Casey had taken several items of Caylee's clothing to the apartment of a nanny who cared for Caylee from 2006 to 2008, and that the nanny had purchased several items of clothing for Caylee during that time period.

Despite widespread belief that there was no real "nanny" who cared for Caylee, and that Casey lied about where she was bringing Caylee when she said she was taking her to the "nanny," there's no doubt that Casey regularly took the child *someplace* to be with *someone* for *some* purpose because numerous witnesses described being with Casey on occasions when the child was not present *and* was not with George or Cindy. One of those times, according to Casey, was the last day that Caylee was seen alive. Casey told George she was bringing Caylee to stay with the "nanny" and that when she went to retrieve Caylee the next day, June 17, at Sawgrass Apartments where she said the "nanny" lived, both the child and the "nanny" were gone. Police said Casey lied about the "nanny," but they did not say she lied about regularly bringing the child *someplace*. We need to ask whether evidence corroborates Casey's claim that a "nanny" kidnapped her child. What actions did Casey take around the time of the alleged kidnapping? Do they confirm or rebut her claims about a kidnapping?

Casey's Activities on June 16th and 17th

Casey's cell phone and "ping" records reveal that on the 16th and 17th, she spent a lot of time with, and/or on the phone talking to, Tony Lazzaro, Amy Huizenga and Ricardo Morales. (See Exhibit 4) Cindy testified in her deposition that the investigator she hired, Dominic Casey, found out that Tony Lazzaro was involved in an "entertainment" business that had a corporate lease at Sawgrass Apartments and that the company rented several units there. (See Exhibit 5). Despite many seeming connections between Casey and the Sawgrass Apartments, including the simple fact that Casey's friend Annie Downing told cops that Casey visited her often when Annie lived there in 2006 and 2007, the manager of Sawgrass testified at trial that she had never seen Casey at the premises.

Tony Lazzaro left Florida for New York on June 30th, 2008. Ricardo and Amy went to Puerto Rico, along with a guy named J.P. Chatt, on July 2nd. They all returned to Florida in July and submitted to questioning by police, but the transcripts of their interviews are oddly lacking in robust questions about some of the basics.

For example, there's little discussion of how they all know each other, even though Cindy testified about being told by law enforcement of a "connection" between Tony, Ricardo and Amy, and that this "connection" was the focus of an interview between herself and the FBI—and not all of the FBI transcripts have been released. She also testified that the Orlando Police told George some of Casey's friends were under FBI surveillance and that a man named "Scott Bolin" at the FBI in Leesburg told her that Amy and Ricardo had criminal records and that both had known Tony "for a long time." Lee testified in his deposition that Amy was a serious heroin user.

Casey's Brother, Lee Anthony

In this same section of her testimony, Cindy says that Casey had been told to "keep her mouth shut" or "something would happen to Caylee or ... her family." (See Exhibit 1B). Who told Casey to keep quiet and why?

George wrote in his infamous suicide note that he bought a gun in August 2008 because he wanted to confront Casey's friends about Caylee's whereabouts. Why was George suspicious?

Whether these friends of Casey's know anything about Caylee's murder is unclear, but it's noteworthy that cops were very interested in Amy, Ricardo and Tony. In fact, they interviewed Tony and Ricardo four times each, and had Tony wear a wire for several months. During one of Tony's police interviews, cops refer to "leads" Tony gave them that the detectives "don't want to talk about on tape."

It matters that although Casey blamed the "nanny" for kidnapping Caylee, she spent most of her time in the days around Caylee's disappearance talking to Amy, Ricardo and Tony, people with "connections" to each other and to some "entertainment" business affiliated with Sawgrass Apartments. Is this entertainment business related to Casey prostituting herself?

Whoever killed Caylee, unraveling the mystery of the "nanny" remains important because it cannot reasonably be disputed that there was a *someone* who regularly had custody of Caylee in some caretaking capacity between 2006 and the middle of 2008. Whether that someone was a nanny or not, and whatever his or her real identity, the possible role of that person in Caylee's death has yet to be explained.

I address what we know of the "nanny" in the next chapter.

Exhibit 2. Casey Refuses Immunity Deal Offer

My FOX TV Orlando   Published : Wednesday, 03 Sep 2008

Immunity deal expires for Casey Anthony

ORANGE COUNTY, Fla. (WOFL FOX 35) - The mother of a missing toddler did not respond by Tuesday to an offer that would have given her some protection from prosecution if she told investigators what she knows about her daughter's disappearance. Officials say 3-year-old Caylee Anthony is probably dead. Her mother, Casey Anthony, missed a 9 a.m. deadline to respond to an offer of limited immunity, a spokeswoman for the state's attorney's office said. Under the offer, prosecutors *could not* have used Anthony's statements against her, but they could have used any evidence found as a result. A spokeswoman for Anthony's attorney, Jose Baez, declined comment. Authorities said Monday there was a decomposing body in the trunk of Casey Anthony's car and investigators believe there is a "strong probability" that Caylee is dead. "We're still holding out hope, of course, unfortunately as time goes on and more evidence presents itself, it seems to indicate something else," Carlos Padilla, a spokesman for the Orange County sheriff's office, said Tuesday. "But we still have our hopes up that maybe this will turn out differently." Anthony, 22, faces charges of child neglect, making false statements and obstructing the investigation into her daughter's disappearance. She was released Aug. 21, but a bondsman rescinded her $500,000 bail after she was arrested again last week on charges of check fraud and theft. Investigators believe she used a friend's checkbook to buy items at Target and Winn-Dixie, and to write a check for cash in July. This weekend, central Florida residents continued to search for Caylee. More than 200 people combed an area near Orlando International Airport, looking for clues about the child's disappearance. Anthony family spokesman Larry Garrison said Casey Anthony's mother, Cindy, remains hopeful the girl will be found. "As far as Cindy Anthony is concerned, we are looking for Caylee alive," he said. Caylee Anthony was reported missing in July, about a month after she was last seen. Casey Anthony told investigators she didn't immediately call authorities to report Caylee missing because she was conducting her own investigation, according to an affidavit. But authorities say she has shown no remorse or concern for Caylee under questioning. "She continues to hold the key to this case," Padilla said.

Exhibit 3. Cindy Doesn't Know How Baez Came to Represent Casey

424

1 blaming you somehow for her being in jail.

2   A   Yeah. I mean, at that point, with her

3 attitude on the phone, she was blaming me she was

4 there. And I did tell her if she wouldn't have lied to

5 the police because that's why they told us they

6 arrested her because she was lying. I believe it was

7 before, but I can't say for sure.

8   But it didn't take a whole lot. It was

9 probably the phone call when Melich told us that they

10 had arrested her --

11   Q   Uh-huh.

12   A   -- that he said that she had lied to them.

13 It was either there, or when they came back to the

14 house. I don't know. But I know we were told by them

15 that day.

16   [Whereupon, Mr. Ashton left the deposition

17   room.]

18 BY MS. DRANE BURDICK:

19   Q   Okay. When did you meet Mr. Baez?

20   A   Oh, gosh. Sometime within a few days. He

21 contacted us and showed up at the house. And for over

22 a week I thought he was the Public Defender. I didn't

23 know any differently.

24   Q   Did you hire him?

25   A   No.

22

Date Time	Record type	Calling	Called	IMEI	IMSI	durati	LAC	CID	LAT	125	E.164	Phone ID
2008/06/16 01:15:4	MOBILE ORIGINATING SMS	16319025443	14076199286	0	111	3104	1	27216-21788	28.454722	-81.265611	14047259320	From Tony Lazzaro
2008/06/16 01:17:0	MOBILE ORIGINATING SMS	14076199286	16319025443	0	111	3104	0	27216-21781	28.4547222	-81.2636111	14047259320	To Tony Lazzaro
2008/06/16 01:18:1	MOBILE TERMINATING SMS	16319025443	14076199286	0	111	3104	0	27216-22292	28.5028444	-81.2863333	14047259320	From Tony Lazzaro
2008/06/16 01:19:4	MOBILE ORIGINATING SMS	16319025443	14076199286	0	111	3104	0	27216-21781	28.4547222	-81.2636111	14047259320	From Tony Lazzaro
2008/06/16 01:23:5	MOBILE ORIGINATING SMS	14076199286	16319025443	0	111	3104	0	27216-22292	28.5028444	-81.2863333	14047259320	To Tony Lazzaro
2008/06/16 01:31:1	MOBILE ORIGINATING SMS	14076199286	16319025443	0	111	3104	0	27216-21781	28.4547222	-81.2636111	14047259320	To Tony Lazzaro
2008/06/16 01:54:4	MOBILE ORIGINATING SMS	14076199286	16319025443	0	111	3104	0	27216-21781	28.4547222	-81.2636111	14047259320	To Tony Lazzaro
2008/06/16 02:57:0	MOBILE TERMINATING SMS	16319025443	14076199286	0	111	3104	0	27216-21781	28.4547222	-81.2636111	14047259320	To Tony Lazzaro
2008/06/16 03:03:0	MOBILE ORIGINATING SMS	16319025443	14076199286	0	111	3104	862	27216-21781	28.4547222	-81.2636111	14047259320	To Tony Lazzaro
2008/06/16 03:22:4	MOBILE ORIGINATING SMS	14076199286	16319025443	0	111	3104	1	27216-21781	28.4547222	-81.2636111	14047259320	From Tony Lazzaro
2008/06/16 07:45:5	MOBILE ORIGINATING	14072754909	14076199286	0	111	3104	1				14047259408	From Mobile Hopespring Landline
2008/06/16 07:45:5	MOBILE ORIGINATING	14076199286	14072474896			3104	1				14047259408	AT&T Voicemail
2008/06/16 08:46:3	MOBILE ORIGINATING	16319025443	16319025443	0	111	3104	0	27216-22292	28.5028444	-81.2863333	14047259320	To Tony Lazzaro
2008/06/16 11:43:4	MOBILE ORIGINATING SMS	16977722	14076199286	0	111	3104	1115	27216-22292	28.5028444	-81.2863333	14047259320	From Tony Lazzaro
2008/06/16 11:47:4	MOBILE TERMINATING	16319025443	14076194296	0	111	3104	0	27216-21781	28.4547222	-81.2636111	14047259320	From Tony Lazzaro
2008/06/16 11:52:5	MOBILE TERMINATING	16977722	14076199286	0	111	3104	0	27216-22292	28.5028444	-81.2863333	14047259320	to Tony Lazzaro
2008/06/16 12:53:1	MOBILE TERMINATING SMS	16319025443	14076199286	0	111	3104	0	27216-22292	28.5028444	-81.2863333	14047259320	From Tony Lazzaro
2008/06/16 12:55:5	MOBILE TERMINATING SMS	16319025443	16319025443	0	111	3104	0	27216-22292	28.5028444	-81.2863333	14047259320	From Tony Lazzaro
2008/06/16 13:00:5	MOBILE ORIGINATING	16319025443	14076199286	0	111	3104	829	27216-21781	28.4547222	-81.2636111	14047259320	to Tony Lazzaro
2008/06/16 13:20:4	MOBILE ORIGINATING SMS	14076199286	14076299203	0	111	3104	0	27216-22292	28.5028444	-81.2863333	14047259320	From Jesse Grund
2008/06/16 13:27:0	MOBILE TERMINATING SMS	14076299293	14076199286	0	111	3104	0	27216-22292	28.5028444	-81.2863333	14047259320	From Jesse Grund
2008/06/16 13:44:5	MOBILE ORIGINATING SMS	14076299293	14076199286	0	111	3104	2164	27216-22292	28.5028444	-81.2863333	14047259320	to Jesse Grund
2008/06/16 14:52:5	MOBILE TERMINATING	14074629293	14076199286	0	111	3104	673	27216-22292	28.5028444	-81.2863333	14047259320	From George Anthony
2008/06/16 15:04:0	MOBILE ORIGINATING	14074035564	14076199286	0	111	3104	26	27216-22292	28.5028444	-81.2863333	14047259320	From Jesse Grund
2008/06/16 15:23:5	MOBILE TERMINATING SMS	16977724	14076199298	0	111	3104	0	27216-22292	28.5028444	-81.2863333	14047259320	From Amy Huizenga
2008/06/16 15:35:0	MOBILE TERMINATING SMS	16977722	14076199286	0	111	3104	22	27216-22292	28.5028444	-81.2863333	14047259320	to Lexus of Orlando
2008/06/16 15:39:5	MOBILE ORIGINATING	16977723	16319025443	0	111	3104	0	27216-22292	28.5028444	-81.2863333	14047259320	to Lexus of Orlando
2008/06/16 16:10:4	MOBILE ORIGINATING	14076199286	14076199286	0	111	3104	34	27216-22292	28.5028444	-81.2863333	14047259320	to Cynthia Anthony
2008/06/16 16:11:4	MOBILE ORIGINATING	14076199286	14078084273	0	111	3104	3	27216-21787	28.4547727	-81.2767472	14047259310	to Cynthia Anthony
2008/06/16 16:13:0	MOBILE ORIGINATING	14076199286	14078084273	0			2				14047259310	to Cynthia Anthony
2008/06/16 16:13:5	MOBILE ORIGINATING	14076199286	14078084273	0	111	3104	0	27216-22292	28.5028444	-81.2863333	14047259310	to Cynthia Anthony
2008/06/16 16:14:4	MOBILE ORIGINATING	14076199286	10000	0	111	3104	98	27216-22291	28.5028444	-81.2863333	14047259320	to Lexus of Orlando
2008/06/16 16:18:3	MOBILE TERMINATING SMS	16319025443	14076199286	0			0	27201-21712	28.5444	-81.2767472	14047259310	From Tony Lazzaro
2008/06/16 16:19:1	MOBILE ORIGINATING SMS	14076199286	16319025443	0			0	27201-21712	28.5444	-81.2767472	14047259310	From Tony Lazzaro
2008/06/16 16:19:5	MOBILE ORIGINATING	14076199286	14076199286				58	27201-21712	28.5444	-81.2767472	14047259310	to Jesse Grund
2008/06/16 16:21:3	MOBILE ORIGINATING	14076199286	14074629293				75	27201-2071	28.5444	-81.2767472	14047259310	to Jesse Grund
2008/06/16 16:25:2	MOBILE ORIGINATING	14076199286	14078084273	0	111	3104					14047259310	to Cynthia Anthony

Of these 252 calls, 75 are via phone and 117 via text.

Date Time	Record type	Calling	Called	IMEI	IMSI	urati	LAC	CID	LAT	125	E.164	Phone ID
2008/06/16 16:53:5	MOBILE TERMINATING SMS	132665197	14076199286	0	1111	3104	0	27201-20341	28.5653389	-81.2958856	14047259408	?????
2008/06/16 17:57:5	MOBILE TERMINATING SMS	11	14076199286	0	1111	3104	0	27201-20723	28.6059167	-81.2876111	14047259310	?????
2008/06/16 18:31:4	MOBILE ORIGINATING	14076199286	14078084731	0	1111	3104	0	27201-20723	28.6059167	-81.2876111	14047259310	To Cynthia Anthony
2008/06/16 18:32:1	MOBILE ORIGINATING	14076199286	14078084731	0	1111	3104	3	27201-20723	28.6059167	-81.2876111	14047259310	To Cynthia Anthony
2008/06/16 18:32:5	MOBILE ORIGINATING	14076199286	14077274909	0	1111	3104	17	27201-21512	28.5993583	-81.30325	14047259310	To Hopespring House landline
2008/06/16 18:33:4	MOBILE ORIGINATING	14076199286	14077274909	0	1111	3104	51	27201-21512	28.5993583	-81.30325	14047259310	To Hopespring House landline
2008/06/16 18:34:2	MOBILE TERMINATING SMS	0	14076199286	0	1111	3104	0	27201-20723	28.6039167	-81.2876111	14047259310	Casey calls to self
2008/06/16 18:34:2	MOBILE ORIGINATING	10	14076199286	0	1111	3104	0	27201-20723	28.6030167	-81.2876111	14047259310	?????
2008/06/16 19:06	MOBILE ORIGINATING	14076199286	14076199286	0	1111	3104	83	27201-20723	28.6039167	-81.2876111	14047259310	?????
2008/06/16 19:20:2	MOBILE ORIGINATING	14076199286	14077275409	0	1111	5104	0	27201-20341	28.5653389	-81.2958856	14047259310	To Amy Huizenga
2008/06/16 19:21:0	MOBILE ORIGINATING	14076199286	19543289214	0	1111	3104	42	27201-21512	28.5993583	-81.30325	14047259310	To Amy Huizenga
2008/06/16 20:03:1	MOBILE ORIGINATING	14076199286	14077427286	0	1111	3104	6	27201-20341	28.5653389	-81.2958856	14047259310	?????
2008/06/16 20:03:1	MOBILE TERMINATING SMS	16235209451 1	14076199286	0	1111	3104	6	27201-20341	28.5653389	-81.2958856	14047259310	AT&T Voicemail
2008/06/16 21:04:0	MOBILE TERMINATING SMS	11	14076199286	0	1111	5104	6	27201-20341	28.5653389	-81.2958856	14047259310	From Savannah Carter "aka Mark?"
2008/06/16 22:45:0	MOBILE TERMINATING SMS	19543289214	14076199286	0	1111	3104	0	27201-21512	28.5993583	-81.30325	14047259310	?????
2008/06/16 23:17:4	MOBILE TERMINATING SMS	19543289214	14076199286	0	1111	3104	0	27201-21512	28.5993583	-81.30325	14047259310	?????
2008/06/17 10:52:3	MOBILE TERMINATING SMS	11	14076199286	0	1111	3104	37	27201-20341	28.5653389	-81.2958856	14047259310	From Amy Huizenga
2008/06/17 10:59:3	MOBILE TERMINATING SMS	0	14076199286	0	1111	3104	0	27201-20341	28.5653389	-81.2958856	14047259310	Casey calls to self
2008/06/17 11:05:2	MOBILE TERMINATING SMS	14076199286	19543289214	0	1111	3104	446	27201-21512	28.5993583	-81.30325	14047259310	?????
2008/06/17 11:27:1	MOBILE ORIGINATING	14076199286	14076199286	0	1111	3104	0	27201-21512	28.5993583	-81.30325	14047259310	From Amy Huizenga
2008/06/17 11:28:1	MOBILE ORIGINATING	19543289214	14076199286	0	1111	3104	0	27201-21512	28.5993583	-81.30325	14047259310	From Amy Huizenga
2008/06/17 11:29:1	MOBILE TERMINATING SMS	19543289214	14076199286	0	1111	3104	0	27201-21512	28.5993583	-81.30325	14047259310	From Amy Huizenga
2008/06/17 11:30:0	MOBILE ORIGINATING	14076199286	14076199286	0	1111	3104	0	27201-21512	28.5993583	-81.30325	14047259310	?????
2008/06/17 11:32:0	MOBILE ORIGINATING	1697774	14076199286	0	1111	3104	0	27201-21512	28.5993583	-81.30325	14047259310	From Amy Huizenga
2008/06/17 12:12:5	MOBILE ORIGINATING	14076199286	14076710000	0	1111	3104	190	27201-21512	28.5993583	-81.30325	14047259310	To Lexus of Orlando
2008/06/17 12:40:5	MOBILE ORIGINATING	14076199286	19543289214	0	1111	3104	542	27201-21512	28.5653389	-81.2958856	14047259310	To Amy Huizenga
2008/06/17 14:15	MOBILE ORIGINATING	14076199286	14076199286	0	1111	3104	73	27201-22292	28.5028444	-81.2863333	14047259320	To Ricardo Morales
2008/06/17 14:18:1	MOBILE TERMINATING	18134208750	14076199286	0	1111	5104	460	27201-22292	28.5028444	-81.2863333	14047259320	From Amy Huizenga
2008/06/17 14:29:1	MOBILE TERMINATING	14076447111	14076199286	0	1111	3104	0	27201-20341	28.5653389	-81.2958856	14047259310	To Tony Lazzaro
2008/06/17 14:30:5	MOBILE ORIGINATING	14076199286	16319025443	0	1111	3104	15	27216-21781	26.4547222	-81.26.3611	14047259320	To Tony Lazzaro
2008/06/17 14:44:0	MOBILE ORIGINATING	14076199286	16319025443	0	1111	3104	15	27216-21781	26.4547222	-81.26.3611	14047259320	To Tony Lazzaro
2008/06/17 14:44:4	MOBILE ORIGINATING	14076199286	19042371143	0	1111	3104	4	27216-21781	26.4547222	-81.26.3611	14047259310	To Tony Lazzaro
2008/06/17 14:45:1	MOBILE ORIGINATING	14076199286	19042371143	0	1111	3104	50	27216-21781	28.4547222	-81.2863333	14047259310	To Roy House
2008/06/17 14:45:1	MOBILE ORIGINATING	14076199286	14076199286	0	1111	3104	50	27216-22292	28.5028444	-81.2863333	14047259320	To Roy House
2008/06/17 14:49:4	MOBILE TERMINATING	16319025443	14076199286	0	1111	3104	0	27216-22292	28.5028444	-81.2863333	14047259320	From Tony Lazzaro
2008/06/17 15:47:0	MOBILE TERMINATING SMS	16319025443	14076199286	0	1111	3104	0	27216-24105	28.4691667	-81.29.16667	14047259320	To Tony Lazzaro
2008/06/17 15:53:5	MOBILE TERMINATING SMS	16319025443	16319025443	0	1111	3104	0	27216-24105	28.4691667	-81.29.16667	14047259320	From Tony Lazzaro
2008/06/17 15:54:3	MOBILE ORIGINATING SMS	16319025443	16319025443	0	1111	3104	0	27216-24105	28.4547222	-81.26.5611	14047259320	From Tony Lazzaro
2008/06/17 15:55:	MOBILE ORIGINATING SMS	14076199286	16319025443	0	1111	3104	0	27216-21781	26.4547222	-81.26.5611	14047259320	To Tony Lazzaro
2008/06/17 15:55:3	MOBILE TERMINATING SMS	16319025443	14076199286	0	1111	3104	0	27216-21781	26.4547222	-81.2863333	14047259320	From Tony Lazzaro
2008/06/17 15:56:0	MOBILE ORIGINATING SMS	14076199286	16319025443	0	1111	3104	0	27216-22292	28.5028444	-81.2863333	14047259320	To Tony Lazzaro
2008/06/17 15:56:4	MOBILE TERMINATING SMS	16319025443	14076199286	0	1111	3104	0	27216-22292	28.5028444	-81.2863333	14047259320	From Tony Lazzaro

Date Time	Record type	Calling	Called	IMEI	IMSI		LAC	CID	LAT	125	E 164	Phone ID
2008/06/17 15:57:3	MOBILE ORIGINATING SMS	14076199286	16319025443		0		27216 222302	28.50284044	-81.2863333	1404725935 20		To Tony Lazzaro
2008/06/17 16:04:4	MOBILE ORIGINATING	14076199286	16319025443		0		27216 222292	28.50284044	-81.2122051	1404725935 32		To Tony Lazzaro
2008/06/17 16:05:1	MOBILE ORIGINATING	14076199286	16319025443		3		27216 222282	28.5099888	-81.2122051	1404725935 10		To Tony Lazzaro
2008/06/17 16:36:1	MOBILE TERMINATING SMS	15265123	14076199286	0111	3104		27202 220951	28.5705556	-81.2563889	1404725935 10		From Troy Brown
2008/06/17 17:20:5	MOBILE ORIGINATING	14076199286	195447989099	0111	3104		27202 220951	28.5705556	-81.2563889	1404725935 10		From Troy Brown
2008/06/17 17:23:2	MOBILE ORIGINATING	14074213700	16319025443	0111	3104		27202 220951	28.5705556	-81.2563889	1404725935 10		From Troy Brown
2008/06/17 20:23:5	MOBILE ORIGINATING SMS	16977723	16319025443	0111	3104		27201 21512	28.5995585	-81.30325	1404725935 10		To Sean Hickey
2008/06/17 20:58:4	MOBILE ORIGINATING SMS	14076199286	16319025443	0111	3104		27201 21512	28.5995585	-81.30325	1404725935 10		To Sean Hickey
2008/06/17 20:43:4	MOBILE ORIGINATING SMS	19542141187	16319025443	0111	3104		27201 21512	28.5995585	-81.30325	1404725935 10		To Sean Hickey
2008/06/17 20:44:4	MOBILE ORIGINATING	14076199286	19542141187	0111	3104		27201 21512	28.5995585	-81.30325	1404725935 10		To Sean Hickey
2008/06/17 20:45:5	MOBILE TERMINATING SMS	19542141187	14076199286	0111	3104		27201 21512	28.5995585	-81.30325	1404725935 10		To Sean Hickey
2008/06/17 20:46:4	MOBILE ORIGINATING SMS	14076199286	19542141187	0111	3104		27201 21512	28.5995585	-81.30325	1404725935 10		To Sean Hickey
2008/06/17 20:47:0	MOBILE TERMINATING SMS	19542141187	14076199286	0111	3104		27201 21512	28.5995585	-81.30325	1404725935 10		From Sean Hickey
2008/06/17 20:55:1	MOBILE TERMINATING SMS	16977722	14076199286	0111	3104		27201 21512	28.5995585	-81.30325	1404725935 10		From Sean Hickey
2008/06/17 21:27:1	MOBILE ORIGINATING SMS	14076199286	16319025443	0111	3104		27201 21512	28.5995585	-81.30325	1404725935 10		To Tony Lazzaro
2008/06/17 21:36:4	MOBILE ORIGINATING SMS	16319025443	16319025443	0111	3104		27201 21512	28.5995585	-81.30325	1404725935 10		From Tony Lazzaro
2008/06/17 21:37:2	MOBILE ORIGINATING SMS	14076199286	16319025443	0111	3104		27201 21512	28.5995585	-81.30325	1404725935 10		From Tony Lazzaro
2008/06/17 21:59:0	MOBILE ORIGINATING SMS	16319025443	16319025443	0111	3104		27225 207235	28.6039167	-81.2876111	1404725935 10		From Tony Lazzaro
2008/06/17 23:02:2	MOBILE ORIGINATING SMS	16977722	14076199286	0111	3104		27201 21512	28.5995585	-81.30325	1404725935 10		From Tony Lazzaro
2008/06/17 23:26:3	MOBILE TERMINATING SMS	16319025443	16319025443	0111	3104		27201 21512	28.5995585	-81.30325	1404725935 10		From Tony Lazzaro
2008/06/17 23:27:2	MOBILE ORIGINATING SMS	14076199286	16319025443	0111	3104		27201 21512	28.5995585	-81.30325	1404725935 10		From Tony Lazzaro
2008/06/17 23:28:1	MOBILE TERMINATING SMS	16319025443	16319025443	0111	3104		27201 21512	28.5995585	-81.30325	1404725935 10		From Tony Lazzaro
2008/06/18 00:10:1	MOBILE ORIGINATING	14076199286	14072737272	0111	3104	52	27201 21512	28.5995585	-81.30325	1404725935 10		From Tony Lazzaro
2008/06/18 00:11:2	MOBILE ORIGINATING	14076199286	14073807272	0111	3104	4	27201 21512	28.5995585	-81.30325	1404725935 10		From Tony Lazzaro
2008/06/18 00:17:4	MOBILE ORIGINATING	14076199286	14074799999	0111	3104	78	27201 21512	28.5995585	-81.30325	1404725935 10		
2008/06/18 00:19:2	MOBILE ORIGINATING	14076199286	14078999999	0111	3104	72	27201 21512	28.5995585	-81.30325	1404725935 10		
2008/06/18 00:22:0	MOBILE ORIGINATING SMS	16319025443	16319025443	0111	3104		27201 21512	28.5995585	-81.30325	1404725935 10		From Tony Lazzaro
2008/06/18 00:31:5	MOBILE ORIGINATING	14076199286	14076199286	0111	3104		27201 21512	28.5995585	-81.30325	1404725935 10		From Tony Lazzaro
2008/06/18 07:55:4	MOBILE TERMINATING SMS	16977724	14076199286	0111	3104		27201 20541	28.5653389	-81.2958356	1404725935 10		To Cynthia Anthony
2008/06/18 09:01:3	MOBILE TERMINATING SMS	16977720	14076199286	0111	3104	56	27201 20341	28.5653389	-81.2958356	1404725935 10		To Lexus of Orlando
2008/06/18 10:31:3	MOBILE TERMINATING SMS	16977720	14076199286	0111	3104	3	27201 20341	28.5653389	-81.2958356	1404725935 10		To Cynthia Anthony
2008/06/18 10:34:2	MOBILE ORIGINATING	16977724	14076199286	0111	3104	0	27201 20341	28.5653389	-81.2958356	1404725935 10		To Cynthia Anthony
2008/06/18 10:48:5	MOBILE TERMINATING SMS	14076199286	16319025443	0111	3104	0	27201 20723	28.6039167	-81.2876111	1404725935 10		To Hopespring House landline
2008/06/18 10:52:0	MOBILE ORIGINATING	14076199286	14078084731	0111	3104	0	27201 20341	28.5653389	-81.2958356	1404725935 10		To Cynthia Anthony
2008/06/18 12:33:1	MOBILE ORIGINATING	14076199286	14076710000	0111	3104	0	27201 20341	28.5653389	-81.2958356	1404725935 10		To Cynthia Anthony
2008/06/18 12:34:4	MOBILE ORIGINATING	14076199286	14078084731	0111	3104	3	27201 20341	28.5653389	-81.2958356	1404725935 10		To Cynthia Anthony
2008/06/18 12:35:0	MOBILE ORIGINATING	14076199286	14072754909	0111	3104	0	27201 20341	28.5653389	-81.295836	1404729935 10		To George Anthony
2008/06/18 12:36:0	MOBILE ORIGINATING	14076199286	14074035564	0111	3104	0	27201 20341	28.5653389	-81.295836	1404729935 10		To George Anthony
2008/06/18 13:09:5	MOBILE ORIGINATING	14076199286	14078084731	0111	3104	3	27201 20723	28.6039167	-81.287611	1404725935 10		To Cynthia Anthony

Date Time	Record type	Calling	Called	IMEI	IMSI	Dur	LAC CID	LAT	125	E 164	Phone ID
2008/06/18 13:11:4	MOBILE ORIGINATING	14076199286	14072754909	0	111 3104	30	27201-21512	28.5993583	-81.30325	14047259310	?????
2008/06/18 14:05:2	MOBILE ORIGINATING SMS	14076199286	16319025443	0	111 3104		27201-20723	28.6039167	-81.2876111	14047259310	To Hopespring House landline
2008/06/18 14:11:3	MOBILE ORIGINATING SMS	13265124	14076199286	0	111 3104		27201-20342	28.5653389	-81.2955836	14047259310	To Tony Lazzaro
2008/06/18 14:42:3	MOBILE TERMINATING SMS	11		0	111 3104		27216-22292	28.5028444	-81.2863353	14047259320	
2008/06/18 14:47:2	MOBILE TERMINATING SMS	16319025443		0	111 3104		27216-22292	28.5028444	-81.2863353	14047259320	From Tony Lazzaro
2008/06/18 15:16:1	MOBILE ORIGINATING	14076199286	16319025443	0	111 3104		27216-22292	28.5028444	-81.2863353	14047259310	To Tony Lazzaro
2008/06/18 15:16:5	MOBILE ORIGINATING	14076199286	16319025443	0	111 3104	3	27216-21781	28.4547222	-81.2656111	14047259320	To Tony Lazzaro
2008/06/18 15:42:1	MOBILE ORIGINATING SMS	16319025443	16319025443	0	111 3104		27216-21781	28.4547222	-81.2656111	14047259320	From Tony Lazzaro
2008/06/18 15:42:4	MOBILE ORIGINATING	14076199286	16319025443	0	111 3104	115	27216-21781	28.4547222	-81.2656111	14047259320	To Tony Lazzaro
2008/06/18 16:10:3	MOBILE ORIGINATING	14076199286	19545289214	0	111 3104		27201-20135	28.5280556	-81.2486111	14047259310	To Amy Huzienga
2008/06/18 16:11:0	MOBILE ORIGINATING	14076199286	19545289214	0	111 3104	95	27201-20135	28.5280556	-81.2486111	14047259310	To Amy Huzienga
2008/06/18 16:13:2	MOBILE ORIGINATING	14076199286	14076710000	0	111 3104	81	27201-21712	28.5444	-81.2767472	14047259310	To Lexus of Orlando
2008/06/18 16:15:4	MOBILE TERMINATING SMS	13265125	14076199286	0	111 3104		27201-20342	28.5653389	-81.2955836	14047259310	
2008/06/18 16:27:0	MOBILE TERMINATING	19046143687	14076199286	0	111 3104	75	27201-21512	28.5653389	-81.2955836	14047259310	From Maria Kissh
2008/06/18 17:17:0	MOBILE TERMINATING SMS	111130100	14076199286	0	111 3104		27201-21512	28.5993583	-81.30325	14047259310	?????
2008/06/18 17:17:1	MOBILE TERMINATING SMS	11113010000	14076199286	0	111 3104		27201-21512	28.5993583	-81.30325	14047259310	?????
2008/06/18 17:48:0	MOBILE TERMINATING SMS	11	14076199286	0	111 3104		27201-21512	28.5993583	-81.30325	14047259310	?????
2008/06/18 18:17:2	MOBILE ORIGINATING	14076199286	14078084731	0	111 3104	456	27201-21512	28.5993583	-81.30325	14047259310	?????
2008/06/18 18:39:0	MOBILE ORIGINATING	14076199286	14076199286	0	111 3104		27201-21512	28.5993583	-81.30325	14047259310	To Cynthia Anthony
2008/06/18 18:55:2	MOBILE TERMINATING	14072754909	14076199286	0	3104	60					From Hopespring Landline
2008/06/18 18:55:2	MOBILE ORIGINATING	14076199286	14072427686	0	3104	60					AT&T Voicemail
2008/06/18 18:56:3	MOBILE ORIGINATING SMS	14076199286	14076199286	0	111 3104		27201-20723	28.6039167	-81.2876111	14047259310	?????
2008/06/18 18:56:4	MOBILE ORIGINATING	14076199286	14076199286	0	111 3104	35	27201-20723	28.6039167	-81.2876111	14047259310	Casey calls to self
2008/06/18 18:57:2	MOBILE TERMINATING SMS	0	14076199286	0	111 3104		27201-21512	28.5993583	-81.30325	14047259310	?????
2008/06/18 18:57:4	MOBILE ORIGINATING	14076199286	14072754909	0	111 3104	157	27201-21512	28.5993583	-81.30325	14047259310	To Hopespring House landline

Exhibit 5. Cindy's Deposition about Tony Lazzaro in the "Entertainment Business"

1 of it.

2   Q   Okay.

3   A   Lost his faith because of it.

4   Q   In God?

5   A   Uh-huh.

6   Q   [Pause]

7   A   Now, if you ask me should I have taken Lee?

8 Yes. I would say absolutely.

9   Q   Okay.

10   A   Looking back.

11   Q   How were you all with Casey when she was a

12 teenager and wanted to date? How would you have

13 characterized your relationship at that point? Were

14 you strict?

15   A   Yeah. She had to wait until she was 16. And

16 actually it went pretty smooth because everybody that

17 she -- well, she dated her first person that she dated

18 for over a year and --

19   Q   At the age of 16?

20   A   Yeah.

21   Q   Okay.

22   A   And, you know, we got to meet him and we

23 liked him. And, you know, so -- we got to meet his

24 family and liked the family. So it was -- it was okay.

25   Q   All right.

98

1 time?

2   A   No. I'm not really good with names of people

3 that I don't see all the time.

4   Q   Sure. Do you believe or did you learn

5 through some other source that he is affiliated with

6 this entertainment group?

7   A   Society Entertainment?

8   Q   Society Entertainment?

9   A   Yes. I -- that's what I was told.

10   Q   All right. Do you know if any of those

11 individuals have a connection to the Sawgrass

12 Apartments?

13   A   I was told they did.

14   Q   Okay. Tell me what you were told --

15   A   What I was --

16   Q   -- and by whom.

17   A   What I was told through Mr. Casey is that

18 Society Entertainment had a corporate account or a

19 lease at Sawgrass Apartments.

20   Q   Uh-huh.

21   A   And they actually had two or three

22 apartments --

23   Q   Okay.

24   A   -- is what I was told.

25   Q   Did you ever attempt to contact any of these

Exhibit 5. Cindy's Deposition about Lazzaro in the "Entertainment Business" (end)

1   individuals yourself?

2   A   No.   The only person that I spoke with on the

3   phone was Tony.

4   Q   Tony Lazzaro?

5   A   Lazzaro.   Right.

6   Q   Okay.

7   A   I spoke with him once on the phone and that

8   was, like, a week after Casey was incarcerated.

9   Q   All right.   When was it that you found out

10 that Society Entertainment had some affiliation with

11 Sawgrass Apartments?

12   A   I can't tell you exactly when.   It was

13 sometime probably September/October, if I had a rough

14 estimate.

15   Q   All right.

16   A   I can't say for sure.

17   Q   Do you --

18   A   But it was last fall.

19   Q   All right.   Do you believe that you learned

20 that during a period of time when Casey, your daughter,

21 was out of custody?

22   A   I can't say whether or not that was the case.

23   Q   Did you ask her about those people?

24   A   Actually, no.

25   Q   Why not?

Sawgrass Apartments

**Where Casey Said "Zanny the Nanny" Lived
and Out of Which the "Entertainment
Business" Was Reported as Operating**

3 Is There a Real "Zanny the Nanny"?

Both sides at the criminal trial talked about Casey's lies and how her story about "Zanny the Nanny" was the biggest whopper of them all. Baez blamed her lies on mental health issues tied to her experience as a child sexual abuse victim. I think the theory went something like this: Casey handled life's problems by lying because that's what people do when they suffer trauma from sexual abuse.

It's true that trauma can make people act in ways that make no sense, but it's also possible that Casey was not lying about the existence of a person she knew as "Zanny the Nanny" and that this is the person to whom Casey brought the child, regularly, between 2006 and 2008.

The "Zanny" Mystery Unfolds

While trauma can cause people to do and say things that might seem irrational to the ordinary observer, it's also true that Jose Baez had to come up with *something* to explain not only why Casey would have failed to report Caylee missing for a month, but also why she would *then* try to justify her behavior by claiming that a completely fictitious person named "Zanny the Nanny" kidnapped her child. Without some gigantic trauma, the jury might not believe that Casey suffered the kind of emotional distress that would have rendered her capable of such extremely irrational behavior. Being raped by your father is pretty much the most gigantic trauma imaginable.

Mind you, there is no actual evidence that Casey was sexually abused by her father, nor would it matter one whit even if it *were* true in terms of explaining who killed Caylee and why. This is because even if Casey made up a story about a nanny to cover for her own criminal actions, it hardly explains why Casey would have lied about a nanny *years earlier*. Lots of witnesses heard Casey talk about a nanny—and the name "Zanny" or "Zenaida Gonzales"—in 2006 and 07. Richard Grund, the father of Casey's ex-fiancé Jesse, said Casey talked about the fact that she made arrangements for a Zenaida Gonzales to start taking care of Caylee in 2006. Richard said this in an interview on CNN's Headline News after the verdict when he was explaining how he had volunteered to care for Caylee when she was a baby, but had made it clear to Casey that she needed to find a regular sitter. Casey told him not to worry because she had found a new caregiver, named Zenaida Gonzales.

Clearly, Casey was not in the midst of trying to explain away the disappearance of her daughter when she had this mundane chat with Jesse's father in 2006. What possible motive would Casey have had two years before Caylee went missing, to lie to Richard Grund about having a nanny named Zenaida Gonzales?

Cindy, too, told police about "Zanny the Nanny". She testified at her deposition that Caylee was taken to a babysitter named "Zanny" *two or three times a week* from spring 2006 until Caylee's disappearance. Cindy said she never met the nanny, but she was certain that the child was being taken to a woman named Zenaida Gonzales several days each week. In fact, Cindy sent the following in an email to her brother in August 2008, responding to his criticism that the family was in denial because they believed Casey's claims about a nanny:

"You are so fixated on the sitter, get over the sitter. Just because I have no pictures of her, it doesn't mean she doesn't exist. I do have pictures of the apartment, I've given things that belong to the sitter to the police." (See Exhibit 6A).

Mind you, the name Zenaida Gonzales isn't exactly unusual, but the point is, the name was out there long before Casey needed a cover story. The nanny, whatever her name, clearly kept a very low profile because several people who knew Casey said they had heard about but never actually *met* the person who took care of Caylee.

It's hard to accept the claim that "Zanny" was a complete fiction because even Caylee, herself, reportedly talked about "Zanny" to her grandparents, George and Cindy.

Cindy testified in her deposition that she and Caylee talked about Zanny when they had conversations about things like "Zanny's dog." (See Exhibit 6B). And at trial, George described a conversation he had with Caylee on June 16, 2008—right before Caylee left with Casey on the last day the child was seen alive. Here's what he said:

> "I remember Caylee coming out from Casey's room". [describes what she's wearing]
>
> "I said, 'where you going'"?
>
> "She says, 'going with mommy'."
>
> "I said, 'really—where you going'?"
>
> "She says, 'I'm going to see Zanny'?"
>
> "I said, 'really—great'. I'm just excited knowing she's happy and I can see excitement in her ...."

[Casey was not present for this conversation with Caylee. George notes that Casey came out of her room "a few minutes later."]

Naysayers will claim that Caylee talked about "Zanny" to George and Cindy only because Casey told her child what to say. But Caylee was not quite three years-old when she told George she was "going to see Zanny." And she said it—according to George—"excitedly." A toddler might repeat a statement upon command from a parent, but they can't credibly fake an emotional connection between a lie and a real feeling of "excitement." Whatever one thinks about Casey making the child lie about a "Zanny," there's no way she also made the child lie to Cindy about "Zanny's dog". What would have been Casey's motive to create a fake dog? How does one persuade a two year-old to have a casual chat with her grandmother, credibly, about a fake dog?

Arguably the best evidence that there actually *is* a "Zanny the Nanny" is the fact that a real "Zenaida Gonzales" filed a defamation lawsuit against Casey soon after it was reported that Casey told cops Caylee had been kidnapped by a person with the same name.

Put aside for the moment that there are many people with the name Zenaida Gonzales in the state of Florida, and that no living soul ever believed the "Zenaida Gonzales" who sued Casey actually *did* kidnap Caylee. Casey never once said *the* "Zenaida Gonzales" who sued her was, in fact, the kidnapper.

This means one of two things is likely true. Either 1) the law changed at some point and it is now possible to slander a *name* rather than a *person*, (absurdly impossible) or 2) the dopey lawsuit was filed to dupe the public into believing, falsely, that there was never a "Zanny the Nanny".

My money's on the latter explanation, which leaves at least one important question: Why was so much effort exerted, especially in the court of public opinion, to make it appear as though the nanny never existed? Was Casey telling the truth about the nanny kidnapping Caylee? Were people protecting the nanny by making her seem fictitious?

Exhibit 6A Cindy's Email to her Brother about Photos of Zanny's Apartment

Cindy to brother Rick:

Date: Wed, 20 Aug 2008 20:57:17 -0700 (PDT)
From: **cindy anthony** <cindymant@yahoo.com>
Reply-To: cindymant@yahoo.com
Subject: Re: Won't do Greta.
To: RickA1P@aol.com

... I've told you, you do not know the facts. You are so fixated on the sitter, get over the sitter. Just because I have no pictures of her, it doesn't mean she doesn't exist. I do have pictures of the apartment, Iv'e [sic] given things that belong to the sitter to the police.

Exhibit 6B. Cindy Testifies about "Zanny's Dog"

1 by name?

2   A   She didn't talk about Zanny, but she talked

3 about Zanny's dog. I remember probably February Caylee

4 came home with some scratches and I asked her about it.

5 And then Casey told me it was Zanny's dog, so I talked

6 about -- I asked Caylee what color the dog was and she

7 said it was white. And I didn't remember what the

8 name --

9   Q   Did she know her colors?

10   A   She knew her colors. Caylee knew how to

11 count. Caylee could count in Spanish up to 20.

12   Q   Uh-huh.

13   A   Yeah. She knew her colors.

14   Q   Consistently?

15   A   Yeah. Yeah. Probably from the time she was

16 two. She liked to color. We always talked about

17 colors. Casey was reading when she was three.

18   Q   Okay.

19   A   And I was working on that with Caylee.

20   Q   All right. So she -- did she say Zanny's dog

21 or did she respond to questions?

22   A   Puppy. She referred --

23   Q   Did she use the word, Zanny?

24   A   She referred to puppy. She didn't say Zanny,

25 but when I asked her about Zanny's puppy, I asked her

37

Exhibit 6B Cindy Testifies about "Zanny's Dog"
(end)

1 questions about the dog, she would answer.

2   Q   Okay. But you've never heard or never heard

3 Caylee --

4   A   Say Zanny?

5   Q   -- say the word, Zanny?

6   A   No.

7   Q   All right. How about if you mentioned Zanny?

8 Like, if you said Zanny's dog, what you're saying is

9 she --

10   A   She would answer --

11   Q   -- she exhibited signs of recognition of --

12   A   Absolutely.

13   Q   -- dog --

14   A   Yes.

15   Q   -- and answered questions about dog?

16   A   The dog specifically, yes.

17   Q   All right. Did you ever separate out Zanny

18 from some other sort of object so that you --

19   A   No.

20   Q   -- yourself --

21   A   Not really.

22   Q   -- could say that Caylee exhibited a

23 recognition of the name, Zanny?

24   A   No. I didn't need to. Because if we were

25 driving and she saw a black car, an HHR, she'd say "Jo-

4   Where Was Casey Taking Caylee in the Middle of the Night?

Several witnesses described occasions in early 2008 when Caylee was sleeping with Casey at a friend's apartment and Casey would take Caylee to unknown locations in the middle of the night. Casey would rouse Caylee from sleep and deliver her somewhere, then return to her friend's apartment, alone, and go back to sleep. (See Exhibits 7A & 7B). She said she brought Caylee to her mother's house on one occasion, but it has been reported that Casey never brought Caylee to her mother's home in the middle of the night.

Unknown Locations and Sinister Activity

Casey also delivered Caylee to unknown locations on other occasions when she claimed to be bringing the child to a "nanny." Where did she bring her child? Why? This is the kind of evidence that allows for a reasonable inference of sinister activity simply because of the secrecy around something as benign as a child going to a babysitter. It isn't enough to say, "Casey lied about the nanny", because this doesn't explain exactly what she lied about. The limited evidence revealed to the public so far indicates there was a someone who had intermittent and consistent access to Caylee for almost two years. These facts have not been rebutted by even weak evidence that the child was someplace *other than* with a person, whatever her name, who was referred to as "Zanny" or Zenaida Gonzales, though the circumstances surrounding this person's involvement in Caylee's life remain unclear.

As for other occasions when Casey took Caylee to suspicious locations, you can't even use your wildest imagination to make up an innocent explanation for why Casey would take Caylee to unknown people in the middle of the night. Try filling in the following blanks with words that make sense:

While staying at friends' apartments with Caylee, Casey received phone calls in the middle of the night from _____. She then woke Caylee up and took her to _____ for the purpose of _____. She returned to the apartment, alone, leaving Caylee with unknown others because _____.

You can't do it.

The funny thing is, lots of people who are willing to infer that Casey killed Caylee on the theory that there is no innocent reason not to report your child missing for a month, are unwilling to use that same logic to infer that Casey may have been doing unconscionable things to her child when she delivered Caylee to unknown locations in the middle of the night.

The Pimping Theory

One explanation for what was going on, which lines up nicely with the fact that the judge ordered certain photographs of Caylee "sealed" from public view, is that Casey was pimping Caylee for sexual purposes. Otherwise known as child sexual exploitation, this explanation for the middle-of-the-night activities makes sense given that Casey was searching the internet for "how to make chloroform". Chloroform is popular with people who sexually exploit children not just because it keeps kids sedated but because it also creates *amnesia* in the child, which means the victim can't tell anyone about the abuse when she wakes up.

These are common features of other drugs known to be used during the sexual exploitation of children, such as the benzodiazepine sedatives Xanax, Ativan (short acting), Valium and Klonopin (longer acting). Physicians will tell you that shorter acting benzodiazepine drugs like Versed are typically given to kids prior to surgery, not only to relax them but also because the drugs help prevent kids from remembering the scariest things about being in the hospital.

Chloroform is a much cheaper sedative than prescription drugs, and it's impossible to track, because it can be made out of ingredients that are inexpensive and fairly readily available, thus easier to obtain than drugs like Xanax. Casey's internet search for "how to make chloroform" may have simply been her attempt to find a cheap way to keep her increasingly verbal child quiet.

Pimping a child, with or without the use of sedatives, doesn't prove murder, but it does change the overall theme of the case. And it makes us ask different questions such as: was anyone else involved? Is this how Casey made money? We know she had no apparent source of income, but she reportedly gave Jose Baez $5,000 as a retainer in July 2008 and had $15,000 in a bank account. Where did she get the cash?

It's not unusual for legal disputes to unravel under the philosophy of "follow the money trail." If Casey were making money off of Caylee, who knows what that may have meant to others who knew what Casey was doing. Did she make someone angry in connection with her "business"? Did she cheat someone? Did she give someone a motive to kidnap Caylee in order to teach Casey a lesson, as Lee said was the reason behind Caylee's disappearance?

Casey's Income and Finances

There's certainly more to the money story, even in terms of explaining how Casey survived without a job for so long. Casey regularly paid monthly cell phone bills of many hundreds of dollars while she was reportedly unemployed. Sure, she stole a few hundred dollars from Amy Huizenga, and smaller amounts from others, but not enough to cover her expenses. Cindy told cops she overheard Casey talking to her boyfriend Tony Lazzaro the day after Casey reported Caylee missing in mid-July. Casey mentioned $14,000 and a "plan." What's that about? $14,000 is a lot of money for someone who doesn't have a job.

In all the witness interviews thus far released, there is no explanation for how Casey could have afforded two months of cell phone bills, much less all the other things she was buying, such as tattoos, nights out at clubs, etc. There's more to be said about Casey's cash flow, and make no mistake, if she was pimping Caylee, she was making good money. The going rate for adult prostitutes isn't very high, but the price goes up as the age of the victim goes down.

The public has a right to know whether anyone—from Casey and her family to attorneys, judges and members of the media—has investigated these issues. If so, why are we not privy to the results? One answer is that investigations related to these issues are still underway, by state and federal officials. The public can be denied access to information if disclosure might compromise an ongoing investigation.

But investigations cannot go on forever. The public must stay vigilant and continue to fight for full disclosure of all information—even if it takes ten years or more—because the "ongoing investigation" excuse is too often used as a delay tactic—one that public officials love to use as a reason to shirk their duties without the public ever finding out. If they delay disclosing investigative files long enough, the public's outrage will fade (they hope), and the whole sorry mess will disappear—without the truth ever coming out.

	Exhibit 7A. Ricardo Morales Deposition about Caylee Taken in the Middle of the Night
DR:	And then she spent the night again with Cas...uh, Caylee?
RM:	Yes. Her and Caylee spent the night.
DR:	Uh-hum (affirmative).
RM:	Uhm, Tuesday uh, I got up to go to work.
DR:	Uh-hum (affirmative)
RM:	I remember going downstairs. Uh, before I left they were on the couch, Caylee and Casey.
DR:	Uh-hum (affirmative).
RM:	And, uh, I just said "I'm going to work." And she said, "Okay, I'm going take a shower," in my apartment.
DR:	Uh-hum (affirmative)
RM:	"And then I'm going to leave." I don't remember where she was going to by that's what (inaudible).
DR:	I had asked you us, if she had ever spent the night at your house without Caylee and you had said...
RM:	There was one time that I can remember while we were dating that she actually started the night they were both in my bed.
DR:	Uh-hum (affirmative)
RM:	Uhm, I woke up the next morning and it was just Casey. Caylee, uh, uhm, yeah (affirmative) Casey. And Casey told me that uhm, her mom had called during the night and wanted her to bring Caylee home.
DR:	Uh-hum (affirmative)
RM:	And so she took Caylee back home and then she came back and...
DR:	Oh, so you never woke up when she got up to leave?
	(Sound of door opening and closing).

12
Morales, Ricardo case # 08-069208GG

Exhibit 7A. Ricardo Morales Deposition about Caylee Taken in the Middle of the Night (end)

RM:	No.
DR:	Okay.
RM:	I didn't even know. When I woke up I didn't even, I assumed Caylee was still there. I didn't know she was going.
DR:	Okay.
RM:	And then actually on July 1st , uhm, the day before I went on vacation she stayed alone. But she wasn't sleeping in my room. She was on the couch.
DR:	She was on the couch? But that was the first time really that she...
RM:	That would be the first time, yeah (affirmative), that she actually got there without...
DR:	Came without her?
RM:	...Caylee and then, yeah (affirmative).
DR:	Okay. So on the, do you remember when that was about, uh, her bringing Caylee home in the middle of the night?
RM:	I don't really know.
DR:	It was when you were still dating?
RM:	We were still dating uhm, but...
DR:	Back in April? Before that?
RM:	I wouldn't be able to say. I would uh...
DR:	Would you find that odd though for her to get up in the middle of the night and leave and them come back or?
RM:	She hadn't before, but she told me her, you know, mom was very I guess, I don't know if it's protective of Caylee, or just wanted to see her a lot. So I didn't...
DR:	Okay.

Exhibit 7B. Lee Anthony Deposition about Caylee Taken in the Middle of the Night	
EE:	...on the counter, running.
LA:	Sure.
EE:	We don't know.
LA:	Absolutely.
EE:	Uh-hum (affirmative)
LA:	It definitely could have.
EE:	Alright.
LA:	It doesn't, it wouldn't make sense to me that it would, but it could have. (Laughs)
EE:	Well we keep running into those statements don't we?
LA:	Yeah (affirmative), I know we do (laughing).
EE:	Alright, I'm going to go through the calendar real quick.
LA:	Okay.
EE:	May. There's nothing really in May noteworthy other than the, the boyfriend situation maybe...
LA:	Uh-hum (affirmative)
EE:	...changed up a little bit. I discussed with you that I was told by Ricardo that on May 31st your sister and her daughter stayed overnight with him.
LA:	Uh-hum (affirmative)
EE:	But sometime during the night your niece, Caylee, was taken somewhere. Because when he woke up your sister was laying in bed next to him but no more child.
ME:	(Talking on cellular phone to unknown person.) Hey, we're still in an interview.
LA:	Uh-hum (affirmative)

	Exhibit 7B. Lee Anthony Deposition about Caylee Taken in the Middle of the Night(end)
EE:	He said that she told him that she took her home and then came back. Your mother, for me, if, while you're going over this with your mother, if she can recall that's pretty significant. Because if Mom didn't have Caylee on the 1st of June...
LA:	Uh-hum (affirmative)
EE:	Who did?
LA:	Right.
EE:	To me, when he said that that was my starting point.
LA:	It makes sense.
EE:	Because I can go back as far as I want, but that's the first time I know of hey, someone saw this child.
LA:	Uh-hum (affirmative)
EE:	No more child. Where was it taken to stay overnight?
LA:	Perfect. Uhm, I completely understand.
EE:	Okay. Uh, you come up to June 5th . We've already covered this. This was mom, your mom's birthday. You see Caylee at the house but no Casey.
LA:	Uh-hum (affirmative)
EE:	Then you, you travel and your ch...your, you job takes you out of uh, town...
LA:	Uh-hum (affirmative)
EE:	...quite frequently?
LA:	Yes.
EE:	Uh, now we go to the 8th . Uhm, I have highlighted that in red because your mom originally thought in her frantic state that she hadn't seen Caylee from the 8th on. Uhm, but now that changes. We know that to be the 15th . And that's just over stress. There's no finger pointing going on there.
LA:	Right

5 Who Else Had Access to Casey's Car?

Whoever killed Caylee had to have had access to Casey's car in order to put the body in the trunk. Despite what the defense tried to do with experts who claimed there was never a dead body in the trunk, there was overwhelming proof that Caylee's dead body decomposed there for several days. But proof about who put the child in the trunk was lacking, and there was solid evidence that Casey didn't have her child *or* her car on June 17th, the day that, according the best evidence, Caylee most likely died.

Casey's Missing Car

A witness named Christopher Stutz told police Casey was driving Tony Lazzaro's Jeep on or around June 17th. (See Exhibit 8). Casey told him her car was "in the shop". Who had her car? What was Tony driving that day?

A neighbor saw Casey's car at the Anthony home on the 17th, but interestingly, he did not see Casey. The car was described as backed into Cindy and George's garage—a position the witness said was unusual for Casey's car.

There's a door inside the garage through which a person can gain entry to the Anthony home. Witnesses testified that some of Casey's friends had a key or knew the code to the keypad entry system. Cindy said "Zanny" had her own key because Casey made her a copy so she could get things she needed for Caylee while she was babysitting.

**1998 Pontiac Sunfire "Casey's car"
- owned by her parents**

Did someone go inside on the 17th and take duct tape, Caylee's "Winnie-the-Pooh" blanket and heart-shaped stickers, so that Caylee's body would be buried with items that would connect the crime to Casey? Was this designed to deflect investigators' attention away from other evidence? Was this part of the plan to "teach Casey a lesson"? Is it significant that Cindy noticed the blanket missing from her house, for the first time, at the end of July/early August. (See Exhibit 9).

We know Casey regained custody of her car by the 18th because she borrowed a shovel from a neighbor that day and the neighbor said he saw Casey and her car at the Anthony home. A few days after the 18th Casey was telling friends that she could smell "a dead animal" in the car and that her father had run over a squirrel. She also said she noticed the smell getting worse over the past several days. If Casey had killed her child and put the body in the trunk of her car, would she have been telling friends she smelled rotting flesh, that the source of the smell was dead squirrels and that the odor was getting worse? No. But if someone else had access to her car days earlier, and put Caylee's body in the trunk during the time Casey was driving a borrowed Jeep, Casey would not have known there was a dead body inside. This lack of awareness would have made her comfortable talking about the smell of decomposing flesh in her car.

It's certainly possible that Casey made the statement about "dead squirrels" knowing her child's body was in the trunk, but how would talking about smelling a dead animal help deflect suspicion away from her as her daughter's killer? One could argue she was planning her future defense strategy by making a record of the dead animal smell so she could claim that a guilty person would never say such a thing. But that's a lot of foresight for a 22 year-old with no experience covering tracks in a murder case. Wouldn't Casey have thought it a *much* better strategy, if she *were* guilty and *did* know a dead body was in the trunk, simply *not to tell* people that her car smelled like rotting flesh?

Casey Abandons Her Car

Casey abandoned her car next to a dumpster in a parking lot behind a mall, the so-called "Amscot" lot, on June 27th. The car was pushed there by Casey and a couple of strangers after it ran out of gas on a nearby street. Casey called Tony Lazzaro to pick her up.

If she did kill her child, would it have make sense for Casey to leave what was effectively the "crime scene" in such a public location—and then have an eyewitness come to the scene to give her a ride? And isn't it interesting how Casey kept running out of gas? Her car had no such problem before Caylee disappeared. (See Exhibit 10). But on June 17th she was driving Tony's Jeep and telling people her car was in the shop. Could someone have adjusted the gas gauge when she didn't have her car so it would look like the car had gas when in fact it was empty? Could this have been a ruse that enabled someone to have access to Casey's car so that the body could be hidden in the trunk, then later removed and taken to a swampy grave without Casey's knowledge?

	Exhibit 8. Christopher Stutz deposition about Casey Driving Tony's Jeep
YM:	And Caylee was with her?
CS:	Caylee was with her and my parents saw her and uh, started interacting with them.
YM:	Uh, also it says here June 17th uh, a dark colored Jeep Cherokee with New York plates uh...
CS:	Without Caylee.
YM:	And that was, or how did, how did you see her? Did she come to your house with that or?
CS:	Yeah (affirmative), she drove over. Uhm, I had say her I think it was the right before I saw her just randomly and so she decided to stop by the next day. We didn't really hang out or anything like that.
YM:	How sure are you that it was June 17th ?
CS:	I'm pretty sure. My mother and I went over it because she remember Cay...uh, Casey coming over and we had just bought a treadmill.
YM:	Uh-hum (affirmative)
CS:	So it was either the 17th or 18th , or possibly the 19th . It's one of those days.
YM:	Okay.
CS:	We're sure of that.
YM	Okay, so you've looked at a calendar and you're, you're pretty confident those are the dates?
CS:	Yeah (affirmative), we went over that, yeah (affirmative), because she just bought the treadmill and uhm, she was using the treadmill when Casey came over.
YM:	Did she just stop by to say hi? Did you guys talk about her coming over? How did that (inaudible)?

5

Stutz, Christopher/Case # 08-069208GG

	Exhibit 8. Christopher Stutz deposition about Casey Driving Tony's Jeep (continued)
CS:	Yeah (affirmative), probably the beginning of June.
YM:	Okay. Did you ever meet Tony?
CS:	No. I never met Jesse either.
YM:	Okay. Uh, when you say text messages uh, I'm, I'm only going to ask this because I've had a lot of her friends actually save the text messages. Do you, do you have, or have you saved any of those text messages?
CS:	No, I really haven't. I go through about two hundred a day and I just ended up deleting them.
YM:	Okay. So she showed up to your house on June, I'm sorry, your parent's house where you're staying...
CS:	Yes.
YM:	...on June 17th ?
CS:	Right.
YM:	Uh, July 17th, July 17th it says Buffalo Wings with a friend.
CS:	I was with a friend uhm, just eating Buffalo Wild Wings and she texted me saying, "Hey I hope you're enjoying your date," I believe was the exact words.
YM:	Uh-hum (affirmative)
CS:	And uhm, I asked her, "What do you mean?" And she's like, she's there and she came up and said hi and that was about it and she went back with her friends.
YM:	Okay. And you were with a girl I take it?
CS:	Yeah (affirmative)
YM:	Okay. Uhm, who was she with? Do you remember? It says here...
CS:	Uhm...
YM:	...you wrote...
CS:	I think it was Sean Daly and uhm, she said, I didn't see (spelling...)

7

Stutz, Christopher/Case # 08-069208GG

	Exhibit 8. Christopher Stutz deposition about Casey Driving Tony's Jeep (end)
	went out we didn't really go out drinking at all, yeah (affirmative). Uhm, we'd go out and go to a movie and then her mom would call her at twelve o'clock at night saying, "You need to come home," and she'd go home.
YM:	Did she ever tell you what her relationship was with her mom?
CS:	Uhm, she said that she just had a really strong relationship with her mom, but not so much with her dad.
YM:	Did she say why or?
CS:	Uhm, she said that her dad would get involved in her life too much and like try to push his beliefs on her. Like uhm, just how you should act, how you should work. When, and uh, when this whole situation happened where they thought they were getting a divorce, her mom said that you know, we're going to be together and dad's going to be out of our life. I guess that was a lie then.
YM:	Uh-hum (affirmative)
CS:	But uh...
YM:	Did she say...
CS:	(Unintelligible.) Oh, she was talking about buying a house. Uhm, I forget what the subdivision was called. It's by the dump on Curry Ford. Uhm, that her and her mom were talking about going and getting a new house for her and all this other stuff. And she was saying that two hundred and fifty thousand dollars is cheap for a house, which I don't know what kind of house she was looking at but, (chuckles).
YM:	Do you know when this conversation was about the house?
CS:	Uhm. It was actually July, when she came over, or June 17th, sorry.
YM:	Okay, so June 17th, she started saying about her and her mom moving into a different house (inaudible)?

17
Stutz, Christopher/Case # 08-069208GG

Exhibit 9. Cindy Testifies about Missing Winnie-the-Pooh Blanket

1 to people that were associated with psychics, or

2 mediums, or whatever. But this particular tip kind of

3 caught my attention because by the end of July/first

4 part of August, I realized that Caylee's blanket that

5 we discussed yesterday was not at the house.

6   Q   I'm sorry. When did you realize that?

7   A   Sometime the end of July/first part of

8 August, it was not in the house. And when I received

9 this tip from this gentleman, this Luke -- I can't

10 remember his last name -- I had went right to Sergeant

11 Allen with it. And he told me the guy was a crock that

12 had called in, like, the week before and said that

13 Caylee was possibly in South Carolina.

14   Well, this gentleman had told me that he was

15 associated with a group of people that do specific

16 investigations on missing people, and he worked

17 specifically with the FBI, and he was from Virginia.

18 And he was a group of, like, five or six people. They

19 were ex-law-enforcement officers. There was a person

20 that had psychic abilities, but they didn't -- he

21 didn't really call her a psychic, and that had private-

22 investigator skills. And he was kind of like the

23 coordinator.

24   And the one thing that he told me when he

25 called me was that he was pretty confident that Caylee

56

Exhibit 10. Cindy Testifies about What Casey Told Her about Casey's Car Running out of Gas

1   Q   Uh-huh.

2   A   I think I asked her -- I'm probably sure I

3 asked her where she last left the car. And we had

4 already known from the report from Johnson's that --

5   Q   Uh-huh.

6   A   -- it was at Amscot. But I don't remember

7 recalling asking her specific questions of why she left

8 it, if she ran out of gas or anything like that.

9   Q   Okay. And during the drive?

10   A   During the drive. But I -- she did -- she

11 was aware that we found the car and the condition of

12 the car.

13   Q   But you don't remember anything she said to

14 you about --

15   A   No.

16   Q   -- I ran -- you know: I ran out of gas; I

17 called Tony; I planned to go back and get it, any of

18 that? Nothing?

19   A   You know, I -- she may have, but I can't

20 remember. Again, most of what my memory stands out in

21 my mind was the discussion regarding Caylee. There's

22 certain things that will stick --

23   Q   Uh-huh. More important.

24   A   Yes. I mean, we possibly talked about that,

25 but again, my whole focus was on Caylee. I could give

Cindy in Pool with Caylee

6 Did Cindy and George Lie?

Of course they did.

Though shameful, and indeed, criminal, it's never a surprise when a parent lies to protect their child, even if it means hurting the interests of their grandchild.

Juries don't like it, but they understand.

Cindy and George are sympathetic people—parents of a seemingly "bad seed" child who couldn't get her life on track, dropped out of high school and became pregnant as a teenager. They came across at trial as irritated by, but also concerned about, their only daughter. Both George and Cindy were appropriately emotional at the right times during much of her testimony, and it was abundantly clear that they also loved Caylee—their only grandchild—very much.

But they clearly lied to help Casey.

Cindy and George at the trial

The Lies Begin

Cindy said that *she* was the one conducting computer searches for chloroform even though her work records showed she wasn't home at the time the searches were done. Cindy provided laughable cover for the chloroform searches, saying she was actually looking for the word "chlorophyll" because she was worried about her dogs eating certain plants. (She said all this with a straight face).

The prosecutor missed a chance to hammer home Cindy's lie about searching for the word "chloroform" only after being *directed* to the word by her computer after she searched for the word "chlorophyll". Computer experts found that someone actually typed in "chloraform" at one point on this computer—a misspelled version of the word. A computer search engine wouldn't likely send a user to search for a word that doesn't exist. Casey, however, a high school dropout, might have misspelled chloroform in her attempts to learn how to make the stuff.

We also know Cindy lied because as sincere and compelling as she was during the 911 call when she screamed about smelling a "dead body" in Casey's car, she also changed her tune on that issue a few days later, claiming the smell was from rotting pizza.

When a defendant lies, juries tend to use it as "consciousness of guilt" evidence, which they perceive as additional proof that the charges are true because, they reason, only guilty criminals lie. When a defendant's mother lies, juries tend to feel the same way. They think: *Cindy loves her daughter. Cindy would do anything for her daughter, therefore Cindy would lie for her daughter—but only if Casey were guilty because if she were innocent, lies would be unnecessary.* This was the key strategic flaw in the defense tactic of blaming Cindy for the chloroform searches. It was so obvious to most of us that Cindy was lying, it made Casey look more guilty. Didn't Baez check her work records before trial? It would have been malpractice not to do so. Which leaves the possibility that Baez wanted jurors to think Cindy was a liar, and that she was involved in a cover up.

That this whole portion of the trial was pure drama was evidenced by the fact that Cindy's lie on the stand was essentially irrelevant, or at least redundant. By the time her work records were admitted to prove once and for all that she couldn't have done the searches, it had already been made clear to the jury that Casey was the one researching chloroform because whatever Cindy *did* search for, she admitted under oath that she never once typed in the phrase "how to make chloroform."

Did the Lies Continue?

The parade of Anthony family liars continued when George claimed he didn't have a romantic relationship with a woman who helped search for Caylee before her remains were found. He apparently spent a great deal of time with her—and admitted sending a text message that read "I need you in my life," but George insisted it was not a "romantic" relationship.

It might be too strong to call George a liar regarding his denial of a "romantic" relationship with this woman because it probably was only a sexual one—with no romance involved whatsoever. But let's just say the drama on this issue during trial, like Cindy's bizarre testimony about the chloroform, was distracting and unhelpful to the defense.

All of which made court watchers wonder what to make of Jose Baez's strategy.

The defense put on a near comical parade of straw men and women and irrelevancies—propped up as entertainment meant to distort the truth by having us and the jurors look away from any evidence that mattered—whether it proved or disproved Casey's guilt.

That jurors took notes during some of the nonsense confirms what many commentators were worried about when the jury was selected: the jurors seemed a bit short on what I will kindly call the capacity to form intelligent ideas about the evidence. After the verdict, the foreman actually said on a Fox News program with Greta van Susteren that he was unsure what happened on June 15th. He repeatedly referred to the 15th as the date Caylee was last seen alive when even the most casual observer of the trial knew it was the 16th. And then he had the audacity to say he was left wondering, at the end of the trial, whether George had murdered Caylee. Seriously! It's one thing to see reasonable doubt as to Casey's guilt, but there was not a shred of evidence that George intentionally killed his granddaughter. Yet, a juror who had been deemed fit and qualified to judge the case based only on the evidence—and was appointed to serve as foreman no less—wondered whether George was the killer. Talk about an argument in favor of IQ tests for jury duty.

Questionable Defense Moves

The defense should have focused on the compelling evidence that *actually* proved Casey did not kill her child, rather than creating mini-dramas out of vanilla-flavored and sometimes outright false claims about family dysfunction. For example, as discussed in previous chapters, Casey was seen on videotape at a Blockbuster renting movies on the date Caylee was last seen. She stayed in all night with Tony Lazzaro at his apartment. Where was her child? Where was her car when she was driving Tony's Jeep after Caylee went missing?

These are the areas where Baez could have expected to sow legitimate seeds of doubt, but he didn't mention one word about any of it–ever–during trial, and he never so much as hinted at these facts in his opening statement. It was so absurd, I'd liken the experience of watching Baez ignore the most important evidence to what it feels like to watch a Shakespearean play—with a key difference being that the audience watching Shakespeare usually knows the whole truth—while the characters prance around the stage acting strangely because they are unaware of the various subplots. The Casey Anthony trial had a similar problem in that Jose Baez clearly knew all the subplots, but we in the audience couldn't make sense of his strange performance.

Baez opted for an exceedingly perplexing tactic of making the jury listen to silly stories about

George's mistress and Cindy's dogs, all of which may have persuaded the jury to find Casey's whole family guilty of felony weirdness, but had nothing to do with Caylee's death.

Which leaves only one issue: Who told Baez it was a good idea to put on the kind of defense that had jurors confused about whether Cindy and George were lying to *protect or condemn* their daughter?

Baez did pull a few tricks that helped Casey, like delaying the trial with an apparently contrived request to have Casey evaluated for competency, which caused just enough of a delay to ensure that jury deliberations would not begin until the eve of July 4. He no doubt knew it would be good for the defense to get the jury's red, white and blue blood flowing as they decided whether to take away Casey Anthony's liberty—and maybe her life. There are only two days in the calendar that defense attorneys like better: Christmas Eve and Thanksgiving Eve. These "feel-good" holidays can add a nice thumb on the scale in favor of acquittal for a criminal defendant.

Independence Day is a good pro-defense holiday, too, because lawyers get an extra bang out of the kinds of points Baez's co-counsel Cheney Mason made when he went on and on during his part of the closing argument about the Constitution, liberty and American values. Mason was a bit arrogant and pedantic in his professorial admonitions to the jury about their duties as citizens sitting in judgment, blah blah blah, but he rightly pointed out that it is a very big deal to find someone guilty of murder.

Baez and Mason got lucky in the end, winning *despite* their tactics, not *because* of them. Casey was found not guilty because the state did not have the evidence to prove her guilt, period. If the jury had voted guilty, it would have been easy to file an appeal of her conviction, not to mention a malpractice case against Baez, by pointing out how the defense failed to mention the only *real* weaknesses in the state's case—evidence that, unlike testimony about Cindy's dogs and George's booty call, strongly suggested that *someone other than Casey Anthony* killed her little girl.

7 Was Evidence Placed "Under Seal" in the Case?

Generally speaking, in legal cases, it's hard to prove that particular evidence has been placed "under seal." This is because "under seal" means the judge has issued an order forbidding public disclosure of information. Simply put, it's hard to know what you don't know. Sometimes evidence is sealed only prior to trial, and it becomes un-sealed when trial gets under way. Most often, however, if something is "sealed," it stays that way until the trial ends—sometimes even longer if the reason it was sealed remains a valid concern after the trial is over.

The best way to figure out whether evidence has been sealed is to first understand what you can expect to be revealed in the first place. When it's fair to expect that certain information will be part of a case, yet the files released to the public don't contain such information, it's reasonable to infer that the information has intentionally been placed "under seal" by the court. For example, every court proceeding has a "Docket Sheet" to keep track of events in the case. In Florida, it's called an "Events and Orders Sheet." It's the court's list of motions and orders that shows all the proceedings leading up to the trial. A sample entry in a docket sheet might say something like this: "Defendant's Motion For Funds to Hire Investigator." The docket sheet would note the date the motion was filed, whether the prosecution filed an opposition, and whether the court granted or denied the motion. All legal cases have docket sheets, which means if one has not been made available to the public, it can be inferred that the court has ordered it "sealed."

Why Are the Docket Sheets and Some Warrants Not Available?

What are the reasons a docket sheet might not be available to the public? One answer is that too much information in the docket sheet relates to material that is "under seal." Rather than disseminate a redacted docket sheet (which would allow for some parts to be disclosed but with lots of sections blacked out), the court sometimes finds it more efficient to order the whole thing sealed, though the judge will usually then find other ways to inform the public about events in the case that are not related to sealed information. For example, the court might make announcements about hearings, and allow the parties to release copies of certain motions and memoranda. In this way, the public has a sense of at least some of the happenings in the case. Releasing limited information also distracts public attention away from the fact that lots of evidence is under wraps.

Other information that should also have been revealed in a case like Casey Anthony's includes the multiple search warrants that were executed. A couple of warrants have been released to the public, but warrants that allowed law enforcement to search the hard drives of computers to which Casey had access have not been released. According to a computer forensics report prepared by Orange County Sheriff's Office forensics examiner Sandra Cawn, a search warrant for Casey's laptop was obtained on July 16, 2008. Another warrant to search George and Cindy's desktop computer (which was used by Casey) was issued August 6, 2008. Where are these warrants? Why have they not been released to the public? Why would a warrant to search the Anthony home be publicly available, but not a warrant to search the electronic contents of computer files?

While the public may not have had a right to full disclosure while the case was pending, all search warrants should be released when a trial ends—especially if the verdict is "not guilty" because there's no chance of a re-trial, thus no reason to continue to worry about unfair publicity or tainting the jury pool, etc. At a minimum, the public is entitled to full disclosure of *whether* and *why* any information was withheld in the first place, and an explanation for why a particular piece of evidence will continue to be kept secret from the public now that the verdict has been reached. This is basic legal protocol under public records laws in all states, including Florida.

When law enforcement and the court system spend the public's money to redress a public offense, the information gathered is effectively the public's property. And because law enforcement officials are paid with tax dollars, the public has a right to know how their money is being spent so they can hold the government accountable. This is why public records laws uniformly require officials to explain *with precision* why a particular bit of information is "under seal" or otherwise unavailable to the public. In light of these baseline principles, all public officials, including court personnel, prosecutors and cops, are obligated to either release information in their custody, or provide a detailed explanation for why particular information is being withheld.

Some will complain that it isn't fair to infer the existence of sealed evidence from the absence of information, which is a bit like arguing that it's unfair to infer a person's guilt when they decline to testify at trial by asserting their Fifth Amendment right to remain silent. The difference is, of course, that there's no constitutional right at stake for any individual when the court system shields evidence in a homicide trial from public view after an acquittal. To the contrary, it is the public's right to know that vests in fundamental constitutional rights—principles essential to a free and healthy democracy. There's no competing constitutional right to secrecy. Nevertheless, it's also true that the court's "sealing" process often ensures not only that the public doesn't see the evidence, but also that it never finds out about the *fact* that evidence has been sealed. The hard part for the public is finding out whether sealed evidence exists. If the public doesn't *know* that a judge issued an order sealing certain evidence, it's almost impossible for the public to request an unsealing. Lucky for us in this case, mistakes were made that, even before trial, revealed the existence of sealed evidence in the Casey Anthony case.

Sealing Shenanigans

A sealing order is typically written in a manner that effectively prevents the public from even knowing that such an order exists, but in a case the magnitude of Casey Anthony's, where law enforcement has acquired voluminous evidence and public demand for information is insatiable, mistakes happen and information gets out. Ironically enough, it was Jose Baez who let the cat out of the bag about sealed evidence when he made a big fuss about it during Cindy Anthony's deposition. Watch in the following section how many times he talks about evidence being "sealed" during a ruckus that begins at page 496 of the transcript where the lawyers are discussing "exhibit 22," described as a page "with a photograph at the bottom." (See Exhibit 11).

Prosecutor Jeff Ashton notes that in a document containing two images, "the top *picture is sealed*."

Cindy then attempts to point out that she has no familiarity with the sealed photograph before Jose Baez jumps on her to be quiet:

> CINDY: "...just for the record, the only document I recognize on this is the—"
>
> BAEZ: "Cindy, don't, don't, don't".
>
> CINDY: "No. I just want to make sure because— "
>
> BAEZ: "Cindy, no, no."
>
> CINDY "We stopped—Okay".
>
> BAEZ: "Cindy, you can't go into anything".
>
> CINDY: "Well, I was cut halfway off and–I'm sorry".
>
> MR. CONWAY: "That's all right".
>
> BAEZ: "Zip it".

What was hidden behind Baez's aggressive silencing of Cindy at that point?

A few pages later, at 503, the topic comes up again when Cindy is questioned by prosecutor Linda Burdick:

> BURDICK: "Did you see, observe her [Casey] gathering up photographs or videos, anything like that, images of Caylee"?

Cindy Anthony on The Stand

CINDY: "Yeah, she—"

BAEZ: "I'm going to object at this time."

BURDICK: "I'm asking for the witness' observations".

BAEZ: "I think we need to go off the record for a second".

ASHTON: "I don't–I don't think we should be going off the record if we're discussing legal matters ...objections. Let's just get the reasons on the record and—"

BAEZ: "Well, it relates to **something that's already been sealed**. That's why I think—"

ASHTON: "Well, if the court is ever going to make rulings—"

BAEZ: "Okay. I understand. Why don't we go off the record. If you feel that you need to put it on the record, then we can put it on the record."

ASHTON: "I don't think—"

BAEZ: "But what you're asking this witness to do, okay, is to go into **an area that the judge has sealed.**"

BURDICK: "I have no idea what you're talking about".

BAEZ: "I have an objection to it right now, and I think that –"

AHSTON: "**Photographs**".

BAEZ: "I think we need to–I think we need to talk about it. I believe we can all agree".

BURDICK: "No. I'm just asking what she observed being removed".

BAEZ: "You–can we–can we discuss this?"

BURDICK: "I know what you're talking about. I'm going to ask the question, what she observed being removed?"

BAEZ: "I think it's–but if I go on any further it's going to become even more clear and—I'm going to be divulging **things that** *have already been sealed* and I don't think that—"

BURDICK: "I know what you're talking about."

BAEZ: "I think what you're doing is **going into an area that's been sealed.**"

BURDICK: "Not as to her observations"

ASHTON: "Well, just note your objection. There isn't a privilege being claimed, correct? " [note: privilege refers to a rule of evidence, such as the attorney/client privilege, that allows a witness not to reveal confidential information].

BAEZ: "Well, I think there–I think it's quite clear to everyone here that area —**that topic has been sealed by the court** and—"

BURDICK: "I know what you're referring to, Mr. Baez. I'm going to ask – "

BAEZ: "Let's take a break. I'd like to confer with my counsel –"

OFF THE RECORD – THEN BACK ON AGAIN AT PAGE 506.

BAEZ: "Okay, It's our position that this is **an area that's going to be in violation of a court order.** We're asking if you guys would like to discuss it off the record. If you don't, and you want to continue and *proceed, we're going to ask that we suspend the deposition until we can get guidance from the court."*

BURDICK: "Is that an objection?"

BAEZ: "Well, I don't know how Mr. Conway feels–well I do know how Mr. Conway feels. I believe he agrees that this is the right thing to do because he's about to have his client—"

CONWAY: "To come back and answer those if the judge says answer those."

ASHTON: "Well, the difficulty is, is by Florida deposition practice, the only question a witness is privileged not to answer is a claim of privilege; and there's no claim of privilege here. You're asking—you're stating an objection. The court can always, if it finds an objection appropriate, to strike or redact, if you will, answered in a deposition. So at this point, your remedy is to, after the deposition is done, to state your objection to the court, have the court redact, if the court agrees with you. There's no prejudice [note: prejudice means harm] to the defense in getting this answer now because it does not prevent you from going to the court and making your point if your concern is–your–my understanding is your concern is not that we will learn something that we don't already know."

BAEZ: "Correct."

ASHTON: "You indicated because we already know this. **Your concern is the public knowing something.** And you have a remedy, which is to go to the court to ask the court to either strike or redact or seal some portion of the deposition. So at this point, I don't believe that it's appropriate to suspend the deposition because the concern is not that we'll learn something we don't already know. So you have a remedy. So at this point, I don't believe, under Florida law, that we're required to suspend in order for you to effect your remedy."

LYON: "Can I respectfully disagree for just a minute Mr. Ashton"?

ASHTON: "Sure."

LYON: "You know what's going to happen is that **this information will make its way into the public wheel some kind of way once the question is answered. And there's a court order that we're trying to obey here.** I think you can certainly infer and know what it is. And I just don't see what the harm is to you in either going off the record and having a full discussion with this, or suspending the deposition so that we can have a full discussion of this with the judge, or simply skipping the question altogether and asking other questions. And you know, we certainly wouldn't object in the event you're successful or that the judge doesn't agree that it would be **violating a court order to ask these questions, that, you know, you can ask these questions**

some other time. You're putting the
—putting everybody in a very awkward
position for no particular reason that couldn't
be delayed at least a little bit.

ASHTON: "I think the problem is, anyone
who would spill the beans if the question is
answered already knows the answer and
could spill the beans if they were so inclined.
But Linda, [referring here to prosecutor
Burdick] it's your deposition. You know, I
think Linda has already said what she wants
to do so –"

[A DISCUSSION FOLLOWS ABOUT WHETHER
CINDY WOULD COME BACK FOR ANOTHER
DEPOSITION]

ASHTON: "Is the defense indicating that
they are intending to file some sort of
motion for a protective order?"

BAEZ: "Yeah"

ASHTON: "So it's not going to be–the onus
is not going to be on us to have the court
rule on this, right? That's what you're
requesting."

BURDICK: "My question was–did you see
Casey?"

BAEZ: "We know what the question was. I
think that what we'll do–yes. We will
represent that we can **bring this to the
judge's attention to make a ruling. And
if he rules that the questions fall outside**

of the court's order, we're willing to come back. No harm/no foul. Just leave it at that."

In this one section of transcript, the lawyers repeatedly mention photographs of Caylee being "sealed," and refer to the court issuing an order "sealing" information about the photographs eleven times!

It's hard to know exactly what's contained in these sealed pictures of Caylee, or what is meant by the fact that the court has sealed an entire "topic" from public knowledge, but in a case where a child dies a gruesome death, and horrific photographs of her remains have already been released, it's tough to imagine that *more* prejudicial photographs could even exist.

Why Are Photographs of Caylee Under Seal?

One possibility is that the sealed images of Caylee depict her in a sexually exploitive manner. It's a fair inference because only particularly disturbing or sensitive images could merit the unusual action of a court "sealing" the information from all public access. Less disturbing images could have simply been ruled irrelevant, but still made available to the public, or returned to the family.

It is significant that photographs were not only taken as evidence, but also kept by law enforcement officials, and then hidden from the public in a file so secretive, that even the *topic* that would describe the content displayed in the photographs has been "sealed" by the court.

It's also fair to assume the photographs are sexualized because of the fact that *search warrants for* computer files have also been withheld from public view. In a case where a child dies in connection with the use of chloroform, which is causally related to child pornography, and where whole files have reportedly been deleted from computers to which Casey had access, a computer search for images of child pornography would have been necessary and appropriate.

The fact that we know computers were searched, but we cannot see the warrants that authorized the searches, or photographs of the child victim in the case, is a *strong indication* that cops were authorized to look for images of children in the process of being sexually exploited.

The public has a right to know what was so shocking about photographs of Caylee, that not only was the judge compelled to seal them from all public access, the mere mention of the topic launched super-cool Jose Baez into a hot frenzy.

Possible Future Actions Against Casey

It's possible that some search warrants remain under seal because the FBI is not yet done with its investigation of some of the facts and circumstances involving Caylee's death. If there is any federal investigative activity still underway, disclosure of things like search warrants can be denied under the "ongoing investigation" exception to the public records law. It's an important if overused exemption that cannot last forever. In fact, good judges won't tolerate the excuse for long, which means a court will one day soon order full disclosure of the entire case file but only if the public keeps up the pressure.

One way to do that is to consistently file updated requests for all information related to the case, with state and federal officials, under Florida's Sunshine Law and the federal Freedom of Information Act (FOIA).

The following two websites provide simple instructions, sample letters and easy to understand explanations about what can and cannot be withheld from the public:

www.myflsunshine.com

and

www.brechner.org

If the official response states that the requested information cannot be released because of an "ongoing investigation," at least the public will have confirmation that law enforcement is continuing to take *some* action against *some* individuals for *some* reason related to the murder of little Caylee. And remember, they can't cite the "ongoing investigation" exception forever. A judge might give them a year or two, but at some point, a judge will rule that they have to either file charges or reveal the entire case file to the public.

Exhibit 11. Transcript: sealed evidence

496

```
1    confer with --
2          MS. DRANE BURDICK:  Can you go and talk to
3    her --
4          MR. BAEZ:  -- Andrea?
5          MS. DRANE BURDICK:  -- out?
6          MR. BAEZ:  Yeah.  Yeah.  I'm going to step
7    out.
8          MS. DRANE BURDICK:  And she's on mute, so --
9          MR. BAEZ:  Andrea, I'm going to call you.
10         MR. ASHTON:  So we're off the record?
11         MR. BAEZ:  Yeah.  We're off the record.
12         MS. DRANE BURDICK:  Yes.  We'll be off.
13         [Whereupon, a discussion was had off the
14    record, after which the following transpired:]
15         MS. DRANE BURDICK:  We're back on the record.
16   BY MS. DRANE BURDICK:
17     Q    And there's an objection posed as to an
18   exhibit that we're not going to ask any more questions
19   about at this point, pending resolution of that
20   issue --
21     A    Sure.
22     Q    -- okay?
23          Also on this page is a photograph at the
24   bottom, Exhibit 22.  Do you recognize that?  [Handing]
25     A    Yes.
```

Exhibit 11. Transcript: sealed evidence
(continued)

497

1	Q	What do you recognize that to be?
2	A	Casey and Caylee in 2007, playing.
3	Q	When specifically?
4	A	Probably -- it was before Caylee's second

5 birthday. Right around Caylee's second birthday, but
6 before that.

7	Q	How do you know that?
8	A	Casey's hairstyle, Caylee's hair and --
9	Q	Did you take that picture?
10	A	Yes.
11	Q	You still have the original, I believe?
12	A	I don't know if it's on the camera that the

13 sheriff's department has. I did not -- I don't print
14 out the -- all of her pictures. Most of them were
15 archived and they're on my laptop that the sheriff's
16 office still has. I'd like to get the laptop back so I
17 can print some of the pictures out.

18	Q	Okay.
19	A	But I'm sure if this was on Caylee's --

20 Casey's MySpace, that might give you a time frame --

21	Q	Okay.
22	A	-- because she usually uploaded it to her

23 MySpace about the same time.

24 MR. ASHTON: And I believe by agreement only
25 the top picture is sealed; correct? The bottom

Exhibit 11. Transcript: sealed evidence
(continued)

498

```
1    one is --
2         THE WITNESS:  Right.
3         MR. ASHTON:  -- not?
4         THE WITNESS:  And just for record, the only
5    document I recognize on this is the --
6         MR. BAEZ:  Cindy, don't, don't, don't.
7         THE WITNESS:  No.  I just want to make sure,
8    because --
9         MR. BAEZ:  Cindy, no, no.
10        THE WITNESS:  -- we stopped -- okay.
11        MR. BAEZ:  Cindy, you can't go into anything.
12        THE WITNESS:  Well, I was cut halfway off,
13   and -- sorry.
14        MR. CONWAY:  That's all right.
15        MR. BAEZ:  Zip it.
16  BY MS. DRANE BURDICK:
17        Q    I think we were in the process of asking you
18   what other items you had given to Mr. Baez when I
19   showed you --
20        A    Correct.
21        Q    -- something that led to a break in the
22   proceedings.  What else do you remember giving to Mr.
23   Baez other than what we've talked about?
24        A    I started to tell you about my hair samples.
25        Q    Uh-huh.
```

Exhibit 11. Transcript: sealed evidence
(continued)

```
 1        A    And that's when Casey asked me if I had
 2    another toothbrush for Caylee and I told her about the
 3    toothbrush that was in the backpack and the one that I
 4    had given --
 5              MR. BAEZ:  Can we stop and -- for a second
 6    and go off the record?
 7              [Whereupon, a discussion was had off the
 8    record, after which the following transpired:]
 9              THE WITNESS:  Because I want to clarify
10    something.  I was asked, on that piece of paper
11    with the two -- that picture that had the two
12    pieces of paper, if I recognized --
13              MR. BAEZ:  Again we're going into --
14              THE WITNESS:  -- the handwriting.
15              MR. BAEZ:  Hold on a second.
16              THE WITNESS:  Right.
17              MR. BAEZ:  Hold on.  We're going into an area
18    that was objected to and I think it's clear here
19    that --
20              THE WITNESS:  But I never --
21              MR. CONWAY:  Tell me.
22              MR. BAEZ:  -- she's trying to elaborate on
23    something --
24              [Whereupon, Mr. Conway and the witness
25    confer.]
```

Exhibit 11. Transcript: sealed evidence
(continued)

500

1   MR. BAEZ: See, we're still talking about it.

2 I don't --

3   MS. DRANE BURDICK: She's talking to her

4 lawyer.

5   THE WITNESS: So as far as I'm concerned,

6 that's two different questions. That's not

7 something I gave to him. I'm sorry.

8   MR. CONWAY: That's okay. Does that solve

9 any problems or --

10   MR. BAEZ: I wasn't -- I was kind of

11 listening but not listening. I was talking to --

12   THE WITNESS: We're off the record still?

13   MS. DRANE BURDICK: No. We're on.

14   THE WITNESS: We're on.

15   MR. ASHTON: We're on. We're on. Perhaps I

16 can suggest that you limit your answer simply to

17 the physical items. Because the question was what

18 items were given, rather than an explanation of

19 why.

20   MR. CONWAY: That's --

21   MR. ASHTON: So perhaps if you could just

22 limit your answer to the --

23   MR. CONWAY: Jose, does that solve your

24 problem?

25   MR. ASHTON: Identify the items and limit it

Exhibit 11. Transcript: sealed evidence
(continued)

501

1   to that.

2   MR. BAEZ: By you. By you.

3   THE WITNESS: That's correct.

4   MR. BAEZ: Okay.

5   THE WITNESS: But I was asked --

6   MR. CONWAY: Just --

7   THE WITNESS: -- two separate questions.

8   MR. CONWAY: So just the specific items that

9   you gave.

10   THE WITNESS: All right. Let's stick to one

11   question at a time then.

12   BY MS. DRANE BURDICK:

13   Q   All right. What items do you recall giving

14   to Mr. Baez?

15   A   Okay. Do I have to repeat the ones I --

16   Q   No.

17   A   -- told already? Okay. So Casey prompted me

18   to think about the toothbrush, so I got the toothbrush.

19   And then when I was in the bathroom getting her

20   Spiderman toothbrush that was in my bathroom --

21   Q   Caylee's Spiderman toothbrush in your

22   bathroom?

23   A   Yes. I remembered --

24   Q   So we --

25   A   -- that she also had a brush where I keep my

Exhibit 11. Transcript: sealed evidence
(continued)

502

1 brush. I did not think about that prior to, so I gave

2 that. Because she asked me if there was anything else

3 that may have had Caylee's hair or a brush. So when I

4 was in the bathroom, I recalled that, so that's when it

5 triggered me to get that brush.

6   So I gave the brush to Casey and the

7 toothbrush and then we took the pillowcase off of

8 Caylee's pillow and I gave those to Casey to give to

9 Mr. Baez. And then the only other thing that I

10 remember giving him was the lanyard that we discussed

11 yesterday.

12   Q   Okay. Did you observe Casey gather items

13 from your home and take them out?

14   A   Yes.

15   Q   What did you observe?

16   A   I watched her put my hair and her hair in

17 separate Baggies. I watched her put Baggies or some

18 things and some things was in, like, an envelope and we

19 sealed it, and she wrote what they were.

20   Q   All hair?

21   A   Hair, the toothbrush, the brush and then she

22 put the pillowcase and a couple of Caylee's hair

23 ribbons in separate pouches. And I had gotten the

24 ZipLoc bags and had gotten them and then I saw her pack

25 those in her bag that she took to Jose's office.

Exhibit 11. Transcript: sealed evidence
(continued)

1   Q   All right. Did you see her remove any items

2   from your garage and take them out of the house?

3   A   No. I don't recall Casey being in the garage

4   without someone with her. I mean, usually someone was

5   with her, you know, wherever she was at, except in the

6   bathroom.

7   Q   All right. Did you observe her gathering up

8   photographs or videos, anything like that, images of

9   Caylee?

10   A   Yeah. She --

11   MR. BAEZ: I'm going to object at this time.

12   MS. DRANE BURDICK: I'm asking for the

13   witness' observations.

14   MR. BAEZ: I think we need to go off the

15   record for a second.

16   MR. ASHTON: I don't -- I don't think we

17   should be going off the record if we're

18   discussing --

19   MS. DRANE BURDICK: Legal matters.

20   MR. ASHTON: -- objections. Let's just get

21   the reasons on the record and --

22   MR. BAEZ: Well, it relates to something

23   that's already been sealed. That's why I think --

24   MR. ASHTON: Well, if the Court is ever going

25   to make rulings --

Exhibit 11. Transcript: sealed evidence
(continued)

504

1   MR. BAEZ: Okay. I understand. Why don't we

2   go off the record. If you feel that you need to

3   put it on the record, then we can put it on the

4   record.

5   MR. ASHTON: I don't think --

6   MR. BAEZ: But what you're asking this

7   witness to do, okay, is to go into an area that

8   the judge has sealed and --

9   MS. DRANE BURDICK: I have no idea what

10   you're talking about.

11   MR. BAEZ: -- I have an objection to it right

12   now, and I think that --

13   MR. ASHTON: Photographs.

14   MR. BAEZ: -- I think we need to -- I think

15   we need to talk about it. I believe we can all

16   agree.

17   MS. DRANE BURDICK: No. I'm just asking what

18   she observed being removed.

19   MR. BAEZ: You -- can we -- can we discuss

20   this?

21   MS. DRANE BURDICK: I know what you're

22   talking about. I'm going to ask the question,

23   what she observed being removed.

24   MR. BAEZ: I think it's -- but if I go on any

25   further, it's going to become even more clear and

Exhibit 11. Transcript: sealed evidence
(continued)

```
1    I'm going to be divulging things that have already
2    been sealed and I don't think that --
3         MS. DRANE BURDICK:  I know what you're
4    talking about.
5         MR. BAEZ:  I think what you're doing is going
6    into an area that's been sealed.
7         MS. DRANE BURDICK:  Not as to her
8    observations.
9         MR. ASHTON:  Well, just note your objection.
10   There isn't a privilege being claimed; correct?
11        MR. BAEZ:  Well, I think there -- I think
12   it's quite clear to everyone here that that area
13   -- that that topic has been sealed by the Court
14   and --
15        MS. DRANE BURDICK:  I know what you're
16   referring to, Mr. Baez.  I'm going to ask --
17        MR. BAEZ:  Let's take a break.  I'd like to
18   confer with my counsel --
19        MR. ASHTON:  All right.
20        MR. BAEZ:  -- my co-counsel.
21        MS. DRANE BURDICK:  All right.  We'll go off
22   the record for them to confer.
23        [Whereupon, a discussion was had off the
24   record, after which the following transpired:]
25        MR. ASHTON:  Back on the record.
```

Exhibit 11. Transcript: sealed evidence
(continued)

1   MR. BAEZ: Okay. It's our position that this

2 is an area that's going to be in violation of a

3 court order. We're asking if you guys would like

4 to discuss it off the record. If you don't, and

5 you want to continue and proceed, we're going to

6 ask that we suspend the deposition until we can

7 get guidance from the Court.

8   MS. DRANE BURDICK: Is that an objection?

9   MR. BAEZ: Well, I don't know how Mr. Conway

10 feels -- well, I do know how Mr. Conway feels. I

11 believe he agrees that this is the right thing to

12 do because he's about to have his client --

13   MR. CONWAY: As to the issue that --

14   MR. BAEZ: As to that issue.

15   MR. CONWAY: -- to come back and answer those

16 if the judge says answer those.

17   MR. ASHTON: Well, the difficulty is, is by

18 Florida deposition practice, the only question a

19 witness is privileged not to answer is a claim of

20 privilege. And there's no claim of privilege

21 here. You're asking -- you're stating an

22 objection. The Court can always, if it finds an

23 objection appropriate, to strike or redact, if you

24 will, answered in a deposition.

25   So at this point, your remedy is to, after

Exhibit 11. Transcript: sealed evidence
(continued)

507

```
1    the deposition is done, to state your objection to
2    the Court, have the Court redact, if the Court
3    agrees with you.  There's no prejudice to the
4    defense in getting this answer now because it does
5    not prevent you from going to the Court and making
6    your point if your concern is -- your -- my
7    understanding is your concern is not that we will
8    learn something we don't already know --
9         MR. BAEZ:  Correct.
10        MR. ASHTON:  -- you indicated because we
11   already know this.  Your concern is the public
12   knowing something.  And you have a remedy, which
13   is to go to the Court to ask the Court to either
14   strike or redact or seal some portion of the
15   deposition.
16        So at this point I don't believe that it's
17   appropriate to suspend the deposition because the
18   concern is not that we'll learn something we don't
19   already know.  So you have a remedy.  So at this
20   point I don't believe, under Florida law, that
21   we're required to suspend in order for you to
22   effect your remedy.
23        MS. LYON:  Can I respectfully disagree for
24   just a minute, Mr. Ashton?
25        MR. ASHTON:  Sure.
```

Exhibit 11. Transcript: sealed evidence
(continued)

1   MS. LYON: You know, what's going to happen

2   is that this information will make its way into

3   the public wheel some kind of way once the

4   question is answered. And there's a court order

5   that we're trying to obey here. I think you

6   certainly can infer and know what it is.

7   And I just don't see what the harm is to you

8   in either going off the record and having a full

9   discussion with this, or suspending the deposition

10 so that we can have a full discussion of this with

11 the judge, or just simply skipping the question

12 all together and asking other questions.

13   And, you know, we certainly wouldn't object

14 in the event that you're successful or that the

15 judge doesn't agree that it would be violating a

16 court order to ask these questions, that, you

17 know, you can ask these questions some other time.

18 You're putting the -- putting everybody in a very

19 awkward position for no particular reason that

20 couldn't be delayed at least a little bit.

21   MR. ASHTON: I think the problem is, anyone

22 who would spill the beans if the question is

23 answered already knows the answer and could spill

24 the beans if they were so inclined. But, Linda,

25 it's your depo. You -- you know, I think Linda

Exhibit 11. Transcript: sealed evidence
(continued)

509

1 has already said what she wants to do, so --

2   MR. CONWAY: You know, I was going to say --

3   MR. ASHTON: -- I think the lecture is over.

4   MR. CONWAY: -- if you guys want to skip the

5 question, we'll come back and answer it later. If

6 you don't want to skip it, then, I mean, I don't

7 have -- I really don't have standing to make the

8 objection. But if it's one question, and it's ten

9 minutes, get the rest --

10   MR. BAEZ: Let's just do it later. I mean,

11 is it really that important?

12   MS. DRANE BURDICK: Who's going to oppose Ms.

13 Anthony -- Mrs. Anthony being re-deposed?

14   MS. LYON: I'm sorry, Ms. Drane Burdick. I

15 can't hear you very well.

16   MS. DRANE BURDICK: I said, who is it that's

17 going to oppose Mrs. Anthony being re-deposed?

18   MR. BAEZ: No one.

19   MR. ASHTON: I don't know that Mrs. Anthony

20 is saying that.

21   MR. BAEZ: He's saying that he would bring

22 her back.

23   THE WITNESS: Well, if I have to come back

24 for something, I'll do it.

25   MR. CONWAY: The one issue of ten minutes,

95

Exhibit 11. Transcript: sealed evidence (end)

510

1   she'll come and do it. You know, I mean, we're
2   not talking about another day of deposition, so
3   that's kind of --
4   MR. ASHTON: So just so we're clear, is the
5   defense indicating that they are intending to file
6   some sort of motion for protective order?
7   MR. BAEZ: Yeah.
8   MR. ASHTON: So it's not going to be -- the
9   onus is not going to be on us to have the Court
10 rule on this; right? That's what you're
11 requesting?
12   MS. DRANE BURDICK: My question was: Did you
13 see Casey --
14   MR. BAEZ: We know what the question was. I
15 think what we'll do -- yes. We will represent
16 that we can bring this to the judge's attention to
17 make a ruling. And if he rules that the questions
18 fall outside of the court order, they're willing
19 to come back. We're willing to come back.
20 There's no harm/no foul. Just leave it at that.
21   MS. DRANE BURDICK: All right.
22   MR. BAEZ: Let's move on to another topic.
23   MS. DRANE BURDICK: I just want to finish.
24   MR. BAEZ: Okay.
25   MS. DRANE BURDICK: We're on the record;

8 What's Up With Roy Kronk?

Meter reader Roy Kronk took the stand during trial to describe his seemingly fortuitous discovery of Caylee's bones in December 2008 in a wooded area off Suburban Drive near the Anthony home. He reportedly happened upon the site when he pulled over to the side of the road to urinate during his workday. Aside from the fact that a meter-reader should have better bathroom habits, Kronk's discovery followed two prior reports he made to law enforcement in August 2008 claiming he'd seen something suspicious in the same area, reports that led to an investigation of the site, but no discovery of the body.

Roy Kronk

Kronk's story is fishy. It just doesn't ring true that the guy happened upon the site and saw something suspicious twice in August, and then just happened to need to relieve himself in the same location four months later. There's probably more to his story—but unlike the defense team's theory about what it all means, there's zero reason to suspect that Kronk was involved in moving the body to that location—or that he had something to do with why the body was placed there, as one defense witness suggested, only a couple of weeks before Caylee was found.

Caylee's Remains

The objective scientific evidence amply proves that Caylee's remains were at the burial site for approximately six months. Plant growth intertwined with the bones can't otherwise be explained unless one makes up a story out of whole cloth about Kronk (or someone else) literally taking the time to knit grassy weeds in and out of holes in the bones to make it *seem* as though the body had been there for a very long time.

The likely explanation for all of this is probably tied to the testimony of Lee Anthony who told jurors his mother Cindy specifically sent a search team "to the woods off Suburban" after a psychic gave the family a tip that the body might be found there.

Hardly proof that psychic powers are real, such "tips" tend to come from people with knowledge about what really happened. Why someone would choose Roy Kronk to be the recipient of such a tip is anyone's guess and nothing has been revealed to suggest Kronk was connected in some way with Jose Baez or Leonard Padilla (the guy Baez brought in to play the role of mouthpiece/rabble rouser and who facilitated the transfer of $500,000 in bail money for Casey's release after her first arrest). Like a lot of people, Kronk knew there was a big reward for the person who found little Caylee and maybe he was just an earnest guy who had a hunch and refused to let it go. After all, the initial unsuccessful search of the area where Kronk first led investigators in August was followed by heavy rains that flooded the site. It would take several months to search again simply because investigators had to wait until the water receded.

Still, it's odd that it had to be Kronk, again, who went to the site in December and found Caylee's body. The search in general, and the strange role of Roy Kronk, makes it almost seem as though certain people not only *knew* where the body had been dumped (no surprise there) but also *wanted* the body to be found, which is weird. Doesn't a killer prefer that there be no discovery of the body? The answer to this curious piece of the story may depend in part on whether the actual killer was someone other than Casey and whether that person wanted Casey to be prosecuted. Such a person would know that without a body, there would never be a prosecution.

If Roy Kronk is really just a regular guy who accidentally became involved in the case simply because he was trying to be a good citizen, why doesn't he sue Jose Baez for slander? Baez accused the guy of all sorts of nefarious things, and all but called the guy a murderer. In addition to Baez, lots of people in the general public have accused Kronk of either moving the body or being involved somehow, but he doesn't seem affected and there's been no talk of a lawsuit. Yet a woman named Zenaida Gonzales, who had nothing to do with the case and came out of nowhere, filed a silly lawsuit for slander even though she was never accused of anything.

It's not clear what all of this means, but it's strange enough to merit more questions. A man called 911 four months before Caylee's remains were found to report a sighting of something odd in the exact location where the body was eventually uncovered. It doesn't make Roy Kronk a suspect, and it may mean nothing at all, but it means we should dig a little deeper and ask more questions about who, if anyone, he's connected to in this mess.

9 The Closing Argument The Defense *Should* Have Given

Because I believe that even the most horrible criminals deserve a fair trial, I was appalled when Jose Baez delivered a closing argument that ignored the most relevant weaknesses in the prosecution's case. He made a few good points, and I liked his avuncular style overall. But it was like watching an old Gilligan's Island episode, where they're on the verge of being rescued if they walk down a certain path on the island, and then Gilligan leads them in the other direction and they fall into a giant pit.

True, Baez gets to claim that he "won" the case – but in fairness to the cause of justice, it's more correct to say he didn't lose it. His strategy had little to do with what was weak about the evidence, which means he is either incompetent (which I doubt) or intentionally sought to ignore the facts that most demonstrated Casey's innocence.

I realize the result would have been the same if he had given a proper closing argument, but it's worth considering what he should have said if his goal had been not only to win, but also to reveal more of the essential truth about why Caylee died:

Ladies and gentlemen of the jury, the state would have you believe that Casey Anthony intentionally killed her child with deliberate premeditation and that she did so in order to be free from the burdens of motherhood, so that she could go out partying with her friends. But let's examine whether they've proved the three things that matter most: motive, opportunity and intent.

Motive

The state claims that Casey wanted to kill Caylee so she could live the life of a party girl. But on the last date Caylee was seen alive, Casey spent the night watching movies at home with her boyfriend. She wasn't out partying. She didn't go out to a club. She didn't go out dancing. In fact, while Casey might have found motherhood burdensome, not a single witness said she was a bad mother, and there is zero evidence Casey wanted Caylee dead for any reason.

Opportunity

Casey didn't even have custody of Caylee on the day she died. The video from Blockbuster shows Casey and her boyfriend renting movies on the evening of June 16th, and Caylee is nowhere in sight. The state would have you believe Caylee was already in the trunk, but you know that's not true because Caylee didn't die on the 16th. When her body was found, it was in a bag with clothing that she was not wearing when she was last seen on the 16th. Recall that Caylee was described as wearing a pink top and a denim skirt. Her remains were found with pink and white shorts (that were too small) and a T-shirt that Cindy said was not Caylee's. Whoever had the child changed her clothes. While it's possible Casey changed Caylee's outfit on the 16th, does it make sense that the child would need an entirely new outfit in the few short hours between the time she left Cindy and George's home, and the time when Casey is seen on video without the child at 8 pm? Even if she changed Caylee's clothes, would she have packed an outfit that the child had long ago outgrown? The bag in which the body was found contained no underwear or Pull-Up diaper. Would Casey have re-dressed the child without an undergarment?

A far more rational explanation for the change in clothing is that someone other than Casey had custody of Caylee on the night of the 16th; someone who had access to the child's old clothes. You've heard testimony that several people babysat for Caylee. Clearly, the kidnapper was someone Casey was not worried about because she appears completely calm on the surveillance tape from the 16th, outside Blockbuster. She told police that when she went to pick up Caylee from the caretaker the next day, the child and the babysitter were gone.

At some point on or about the 17th, Casey didn't have her car. Her friend Christopher Stutz told police Casey visited him while driving a borrowed

Jeep. Who had her car? Who had her child? Whatever the answer, the fact that Casey had neither car nor child at various times on the 16th and 17th means there is plenty of reasonable doubt about whether Casey had the opportunity to kill Caylee.

Intent

It's easy to infer that a person intended to kill her child if she fails to report her child missing for more than a month. But recall that Lee Anthony testified Casey told him someone took Caylee to "teach her a lesson" and that Casey was warned not to call police. Whatever "lesson" Casey needed, the fact that she didn't report Caylee missing for a month makes sense in light of Lee's testimony. The only way Casey could get Caylee back was to stay quiet and not talk to cops. That she then went out partying may seem creepy—but remember, she knew the person who had Caylee. It's clear she'd been bringing the child for months to someone for "babysitting," whether she needed a real sitter or not, because lots of witnesses described Casey as being alone at times when the child was with someone else, not Cindy or George. Casey was comfortable dropping Caylee off because the child was with a person she believed would give her back. Why wouldn't Casey believe this? She'd successfully gotten Caylee back every other time. Who could have taken Caylee from the sitter? Did the sitter know the person? Was the sitter involved? There's lots of reasonable doubt in this case because we don't know the answers to these questions.

We don't know much about the nanny. But there was a someone to whom Casey regularly brought her child for some purpose. Maybe the purpose was something about which Casey feels great guilt and shame. Remember that Ricardo Morales told police that in the weeks before Caylee died, Casey would deliver Caylee to unknown persons after receiving phone calls in the middle of the night. Casey would rouse her sleeping toddler to bring her to an unknown location—then return to Ricardo's apartment, alone, and go back to sleep. Whatever was going on with the "babysitter" and the middle of the night deliveries of the child to unknown locations, Casey was involved in activities that made her very reluctant to tell cops the truth. You can judge her harshly for this decision—you can even hate her for it—but it's not proof of intent to murder.

Too Many Questions

Ladies and gentlemen, there are far too many questions about the untold story in this case for you to fill in all the weaknesses in the prosecution's case with strong emotions rather than real evidence. I know you feel anger toward Casey and great sadness for Caylee. As much as you might want to know more about what was going on with the mysterious babysitter and late night "deliveries" of the child to unknown locations, the fact is, I can't tell you certain things because this is a trial where the rules of evidence prevent me from giving you a fuller explanation. For example, lots of evidence in this case is under seal, which means I can't talk about it, and you can't speculate.

I empathize with your frustration and wish I could reveal what I know about some of the unanswered questions in this case but please know that when you don't have all the evidence that you need to feel certain about what really happened, you have no choice but to vote "not guilty". Who knows, after an acquittal, the state might bring new charges that will resolve some of the mysteries.

Until then, know that your discomfort with the questions you have after being here for so long is not only reasonable—it's reasonable doubt.

There is more to the story—and rest assured—I agree with you that it's frustrating not to know more. You might not like my client, but there were other people involved in Caylee's life who might have been involved in her death. If you don't believe me or my client, heed the words of little Caylee.

Recall that George Anthony testified it was Caylee who told him, on June 16, 2008, that she was going to "Zanny's". Little Caylee was not quite three years old; not old enough to be a co-conspirator in what some have called a completely fake nanny story that Casey came up with to cover for her involvement in her child's death. Caylee was innocently telling her grandfather that she was going to see a person she knew, at a place where she'd been before. Casey told cops this was the same person who kidnapped Caylee and Lee said it was to teach Casey a lesson.

You probably want to know who it was exactly that believed Casey needed to be taught a lesson. I wish I could tell you. I'll go so far as to say it's reasonable for you to believe that even if Casey Anthony did not kill her child, she deserves to spend the rest of her life behind bars because she was engaged in certain activities that repeatedly exposed her child to dangerous situations. But you cannot find Casey Anthony guilty of murder unless you have actual evidence that shows she personally killed Caylee. There is no such evidence in this case because Casey Anthony did not kill her child.

My client may well deserve your scorn and disdain, and if she were on trial for being a bad mother, I would find her guilty myself. But she is on trial for murder—and in this country, she is entitled to be judged only on the facts that relate to the charges brought by the state. The state has charged Casey Anthony with murder, but has failed to prove beyond a reasonable doubt that Casey had motive, opportunity or intent to kill, leaving you with the only morally appropriate verdict — "not guilty".

Caylee and Casey

10 Getting at the Sealed Evidence

After the verdict, the Patriot Ledger newspaper in Massachusetts, for which I write a regular column, sent a public records request for full access to all information from the case file. As I wrote in an earlier chapter, it was clear that photographs of Caylee and other documents had been placed "under seal" during the trial. I wrote about this in a column for the Ledger, which provoked a great deal of public interest.

Readers of my column in print and at PatriotLedger.com wanted to know more about how to go about uncovering the sealed evidence, so the Ledger sent a request to the prosecutor's office in the hope of uncovering the sealed evidence so that the public could develop a better understanding of why Caylee died.

The following pages contain verbatim accounts of what we sent:

July 11, 2011

Office of the State Attorney
415 North Orange Avenue
Orlando, FL 32801

Re: Public Records Act Request pursuant to Florida's Sunshine Law

To whom it may concern:

This is a formal request under Florida's "Sunshine Law", Chapter 119 of the Florida Statutes, for release of information and copies of certain documents related to the recent prosecution of Casey Anthony.

Specifically, this request seeks a copy of the following:

The entire docket sheet in the case, unredacted;

Copies of all search warrants, and affidavits in support thereof, issued in connection with the investigation, whether or not executed and irrespective of whether information seized was admitted during trial;

Copies of all documents ordered under seal prior to and/or during the time of trial;

To the extent information placed under seal is not released pursuant to this request, please release all documents indicating whether photographs or images of any kind of Caylee Marie Anthony were placed under seal and if so, a description of said photographs or images and a detailed explanation as to why said photographs or images were placed under seal;

To the extent any other information placed under seal is not released pursuant to this request, please release all documents indicating with specificity what information was placed under seal and provide a description of said information as well as a detailed explanation as to why said information was placed under seal;

Copies of any and all documents and information indicating that child pornography was sought or uncovered;

Copies of any and all documents and information indicating whether the investigation sought or uncovered evidence of prostitution or any other form of sexual exploitation of any person.

If you refuse to provide this information, Chapter 119 requires you advise me in writing and indicate the applicable exemption to the public records law. Also, please state with particularity the reasons for your decision, as required by Section 119.07(2)(a).

If the exemption you are claiming only applies to a portion of the records, please delete that portion

*and provide photocopies of the remainder of the
records, according to Section 119.07(2)(a).*

*We agree to pay the actual cost of duplication as
defined in Section 119.07(1)(a). However, if you
anticipate that in order to satisfy this request,
"extensive use" of information technology
resources or extensive clerical or supervisory
assistance as defined in Section 119.07(1)(b) will
be required in order to respond to a particular
request for a specific piece of information, please
provide a written estimate and justification.*

*   *   *

In response to this request, Danielle Tavernier of
the prosecutor's office sent to the Patriot Ledger an
internet link to records that had already been made
available to the public. https://sao9.egnyte.com.
She added that the site contained about 25,000
pages of information, along with several audio and
video files.

In other words, the prosecutor balked and provided
zero responsive information.

So I called them, and politely asked them to
comply with the requests in the letter, rather than
directing us to read materials we never requested.

In response to which, I received a telephone call
from another person in the office; a man named
Bill Vose. Mr. Vose left me a lengthy message

advising me that the only information available to the public is that which has already been released. Mr. Vose also indicated that he did not know what a "docket sheet" was and that the only information he could reveal is that which he had in his custody. Information "under seal", he claimed, was not in his custody because it was "under seal." He suggested that I address some of my questions to the court and invited me to email him with additional concerns. He assured me that his office cooperates fully with all public records requests.

So I took him at his word and sent an email making it very clear that "full cooperation" would require him to reveal more information than that which had already been released, or to provide a specific exemption to justify his non-disclosure decision.

Here's what was sent to Mr. Vose on July 19, 2011:

Mr. Vose;

Thank you for your return call this morning.

The Patriot Ledger sent a Public Records request for information to the prosecutor's office, which office would have access to information as to the reasons why information in the Casey Anthony case is "under seal." Your message indicated that the prosecutor is not at liberty to answer this question and that our request can be addressed to the court. You acknowledged your obligation to explain whether any information is under seal, and if so why, but you did not then provide an answer to this very question.

Kindly comply with the law as you stated it and provide an answer to the following questions: Has any information been placed under seal? If the answer to this question is yes, for how long will the information remain under seal? If the answer to the first question is yes, what exception(s) to the Sunshine Law are you relying on to justify the initial decision to have such information placed "under seal" and what exception(s) are you relying on to continue to adhere to the position that such information should remain "under seal"?

Please note that it has already been revealed in public documents that your office "agreed" to a sealing order in the Casey Anthony case. Thus, you cannot now claim to have no knowledge of sealed evidence. Kindly provide a copy of any document or information that pertains to this "agreement" and if you decline to produce such document or information, please provide an explanation for your refusal, as is mandatory under the law.

Thank you.

Mr. Vose apparently took offense to the suggestion that I might actually expect him to either provide the *public* with *public* information or explain why documents that are clearly "*public* records" can be hidden from *public* view.

He again declined to provide the information and sent the following response, in which he explicitly concedes that, indeed, "items" have been "Sealed by Court Order" and would remain sealed "until further order of the Court":

Since you seem to want to litigate this very simple issue of law in another state, I will educate you a bit on the law in Florida:

1. This is still an actively prosecuted case as a portion of it is still being litigated both on appeal and costs hearings, and therefore falls under the Public Records Exemption of FS 119.011(2) etc. Therefore you are only entitled to those already released public documents released as Discovery after being provided to the Defendant.

2. Those Items that were sealed by Court Order are Exempt from Disclosure until further order of the Court. These were the product of 3d Party and Defense Motions that are not disclosable as Public Records per the above Exemption. They are not documents or items required to be disclosed to the defendant and therefore are still Exempt from disclosure.

I would be glad to answer any other legal questions but would suggest if you wish to pursue this further you obtain competent legal counsel licensed to practice law in the State of Florida, and refer them to me if you wish!

Ah, the sting of receiving not only another nonresponsive note from Mr. Vose, but a note admonishing me to find "competent" counsel licensed to practice law in Florida, as if one is required to have a law license to request public records or that residing outside of Florida makes a difference under the law. It doesn't. He is required to respond to all requests, whether from lawyers or not, and he is supposed to behave in a professional manner toward all members of the public, even from those he deems "not competent".

Mr. Vose's sassy tone raised even more suspicions, not only because he was oddly offensive for no reason, but also because he erroneously declared in this letter that "items that were sealed" were the "product of 3d Party and Defense Motions that are not disclosable." He also added that the public records law does not require disclosure because these "items" were not "required to be disclosed to the defendant".

These are interesting claims given that it has already been revealed in public documents that the prosecution and defense entered into an "agreement" to "seal" certain evidence, including photographs of Caylee. Clearly, such photos would have been "disclosed" to the defense. Indeed, "sealed" photographs were indisputably disclosed to all parties as was made clear during Cindy Anthony's deposition when prosecutor Ashton and defense counsel Baez discussed the sealed photos at length.

The curt response from Mr. Vose inspired me to send a follow-up letter asking him to clarify the irrational explanation for his refusal to reveal the information we requested:

Mr. Vose;

We do feel competent to handle this matter, and have read all the relevant cases as well as the statute, but thank you for your suggestion.

You are no doubt aware that refusing to comply with a public records request by simply claiming that a hearing on costs and an appeal from the convictions for lying to law enforcement are pending, is inadequate to sustain an objection to a request for full disclosure of all sealed information post-acquittal. A hearing on costs and an appeal on four misdemeanor counts of lying to law enforcement are not necessarily related to the types of information we requested, which means you are required to specify with precision how particular information you are not releasing must continue to be withheld while post-verdict matters are pending in order to protect a legitimate competing interest.

Note that a hearing on costs has no bearing on our request, and you are free to redact any information that might relate to expenditures to the extent such information is contained in the information sought. Likewise, an appeal on the lying charges can hardly justify your objection given that some of the information we requested, on its face, does not relate in any manner whatsoever to those charges, and in any event, an appeal is unlikely to succeed. Casey Anthony admitted to cops that she lied, she has served the maximum time on all four counts, and her counsel conceded guilt at trial by arguing after the verdict only that the separate charges violate double jeopardy because they amounted to a single offense. On one count, Casey's attorney argued the lie was not "material".

Where the defendant concedes guilt and has already served the maximum punishment, even an ineffective assistance of counsel claim would fail and no appellate court would overturn the convictions. Even if there were a successful appeal, there could be no retrial because Casey has already served the maximum sentence. Thus, as the pendency of a hearing on costs and an appeal on the lying charges in no way justify your nondisclosure of the requested information, kindly provide the materials we requested. Of course, you might opt to assert a new or more specific basis for your refusal to comply. We want you to have every opportunity to lodge all appropriate objections and exemptions as we assess our next steps.

As for your response in point number 2 below, you fail to acknowledge that our original request for certain photographs and search warrants specifically sought the disclosure of information that does not fit the definition of what you describe as "3d Party and Defense Motions." Nor have we requested "documents or items" that would not have been "required to be disclosed to the defendant". Indeed, your office would have been obligated by mandatory discovery rules to provide to the defense, copies of all the information we requested, including photographs of Caylee obtained from computer files, as well as search warrants for computer files and all affidavits in support thereof. As you know, your office released other search warrants and affidavits in the case, which serves as an effective concession on your part that the nature of warrants, alone, is not enough to justify nondisclosure under the exceptions you cite. Thus, kindly provide all such search warrants and affidavits as per our request and note that we can certainly understand that you may need to redact certain exempted information, but the documents themselves are not covered by any exception, nor have you cited any that even arguably apply.

Thank you for your continued cooperation.

Perhaps not surprisingly, I received the following as a final note from Mr. Vose:

You have our written answer to your request, this is still an active prosecution and all of the public records disclosed to the defendant are available without cost to you at the location provided by our Media Information contact.

Alas, we had come full circle. The information would not be divulged without a fight.

At least The Patriot Ledger could take some pride in having been one of the only media organizations in the country willing to publicize the *fact* that sealed records exist. Hopefully a journalist with access to more resources will now take up the task and dedicate the time and effort necessary to ensure that more truth will one day be known.

In the meantime, reasonable people will infer, as they should, that the secrets in this case must be very ugly. Nobody would bother to keep information under wraps after an acquittal in such a high profile case unless the secrets would make the horrible things that came out at trial look like a day at the beach.

include sexual abuse (CSA), physical abuse (CPA), and psychological or emotional abuse. Child emotional and physical neglect are also traumatic, as is a child's *witnessing* of verbal or physical violence, especially within the family, and having a mentally ill household member. Loss of a parent or parent figure through separation, divorce or death is also traumatic.

These traumas can occur under different guises that may go unrecognized by the victim, perpetrator and observer as being traumatic, as summarized in Figure 11.1. on the next page.

Childhood and other trauma experiences are complex. Clinical and research psychologist William Friedrich said, "To simply place a broad label on a child as sexually abused may allow for a simple categorization, but it obscures the heterogeneity [variation and diversity], severity, and co-occurrence of maltreatment experiences." Each kind of abuse usually occurs in combination with one or more of the others, with psychological/emotional abuse being the most common and nearly always present in the background of the other three main trauma types, as shown in Figure 11.2 below.

There are several avenues through which we can explore the genesis and dynamics of trauma and its effects. In the following section I summarize how this usually happens on the process of wounding.

Figure 11.1. Childhood Trauma vs. Healthy Parenting

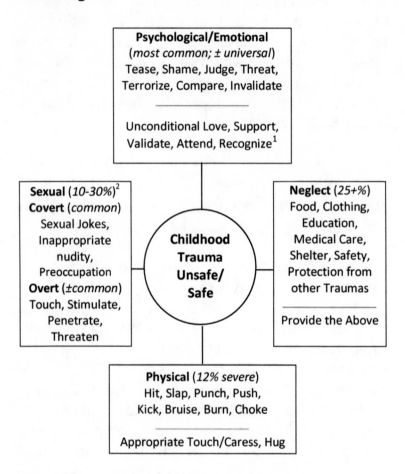

---

[1] Healthy parenting descriptors are shown below the line in 3 boxes as appropriate.

[2] These % figures are estimates of the incidence and prevalence of these types of childhood trauma, based on data from the literature. Paradoxically, statistics based on reports of *child protective services* may show the opposite of the actual occurrence of trauma. These figures are (actual occurrence/CPS reports), *neglect* (25+/50+%), *physical* (12%/18%), *sexual* (10-30%/9%), *emotional* (90%/4%). Most *published clinical and research* data measure trauma in the form of (in the order of the most common study data): sexual, physical, these two combined, psychological and little data are available on neglect.

Figure11.2. Venn Diagram of the Spectrum of Childhood Trauma

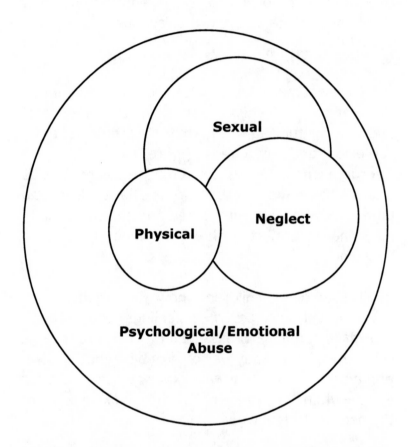

In this Figure, note that psychological and emotional abuse are essentially always in the background and thus accompany the three other main kinds of child abuse. This most common kind of abuse is often *as* and can sometimes be *more* hurtful and difficult to recognize and name than the other three.

If the next section is slow reading for you, please bear with me. Or skip to another section and return later, as it is important to understand the nature of childhood trauma and how it affects us.

The Process of Wounding

1) Previously traumatized and wounded themselves, the child's parents feel inadequate, bad and unfulfilled, i.e., they feel hurt, shame, confusion and emptiness. (Were either Cindy or George traumatized as children? Observers such as Casey's ex-fiancé Jesse Grund have described Cindy's relationship with Casey and the ways Cindy may have projected her unhealed pain onto Casey.)

2) Traumatized children, now as adults, may unconsciously project their feelings onto others, especially their spouses and their vulnerable children. They may also exhibit and project grandiosity (e.g., "I always know what's best for you!"—when they may not). They look outside of themselves to feel whole.

3) In a need to stabilize the parents and to survive, the child denies that the parents are inadequate or abusive. With the unhealthy boundaries that the child has learned from its parents and others, the child internalizes (takes in, accepts) the parents' projected inadequacy and shame. A common fantasy for a traumatized child is thinking that, "If I'm really good and perfect,

126

they will love me and they won't reject or abandon me." The child idealizes the parents.

4) The child's vulnerable true self is wounded so often, that to protect that self it defensively submerges ("splits off") deep within the unconscious part of its psyche. The child goes into hiding (Figure 11.3 below). The "child in hiding" represents what may appear to be a mechanism that helps the child to survive. But the child in hiding is harmed because the child is alienated from the power of knowing and being its true self. The child becomes alienated from present experiences in a number of ways—and from past experiences by forgetting much of the traumas that actually happened.

5) The child also becomes alienated from its inner life—which includes emotionally painful responses to abuse and neglect, such as fear, shame, grief and anger. The child becomes unaware of what is actually happening with others: "Daddy's not drunk. He was so tired he fell asleep on the lawn."

When our true self is in hiding—we are unable to encode impactful memories into long-term memories in a conscious and currently useful way. Yet, paradoxically we somehow store these memories in our unconscious mind as "old tapes," unfinished business, stored painful energy or un-grieved grief, much of which the object relations psychologists call "object representations." [3]

6) When a child is not allowed to express grief in a healthy way, its true self will try to find a way out and express painful experiences, like an enclosed abscess waiting to drain. Unexpressed pain is stored as toxic energy, which may then manifest throughout life as a physical, mental, emotional or spiritual disorder or illness, or more usually as a combination of these. Other terms for this repeated attempt to express its trauma and grief are reenactment and repetition compulsion.

7) The true self continues to take in whatever else it is told—both verbally and nonverbally—about itself and about others, and stores it mostly in its unconscious mind—and sometimes and to some degree in its conscious mind.

8) The mind takes in messages from major and impactful relationships, primarily parents, but also may include siblings, grandparents, clergy, and other authority and parent figures. The experiential representations of these relationships in the unconscious memory that continue to affect these

---

[3] The establishment of the false self (ego) may include some aspects of traumatic forgetting (dissociative amnesia) that are accompanied by the behaviors and responses that allow us to try to stabilize the family and avoid further abuse. As traumatic memory distortions, these characteristically involve a dissociation and/or censoring of some aspects of the traumas, such as the emotional pain of the abuse, and may involve amnesia for some, most or even all of the traumatic experiences, and the substitution of an idealized past for the truth.

children as adults are called "objects" or "object representations." These messages and representations are laden with feelings, and tend to occur in "part-objects" (e.g., good parent, bad parent, aggressive child, shy child, and so on).[4] The more self-destructive messages tend to be deposited in the false self or "internal saboteur," also described as the internalized rejecting or otherwise mistreating parent.

9) Hurting, confused and feeling unable to run their own life successfully, the child/person eventually turns that function over to the false self.

10) A tension then builds such that the true self is always striving to come alive and to evolve. At the same time, the "negative ego" (the destructive part of the false self) attacks the true self, thus forcing it to stay submerged (Figure 11.3), keeping self-esteem low. Also, the child's grieving of its losses and traumas is not supported. Because of all of the above, the child's development is disordered and boundaries become unhealthy.[5]

---

[4] All of this abuse, neglect and resulting emotional pain and confusion distorts and degenerates the way the parents and others relate to the child, ending with what others and I have called core issues, which I address in the next chapter. This resulting "psychopathology" or "lesion" has been called a "schizoid compromise" and a "splitting off of the true self." The outcome can be a developmental delay, arrest or failure.

[5] Children and adolescents need to be given and taught healthy personal boundaries which help them feel safe and allows them to function better. Parents who are loose or inconsistent with their own and others' boundaries are subtly traumatizing their children.

Figure 11.3 The Child Goes Into Hiding

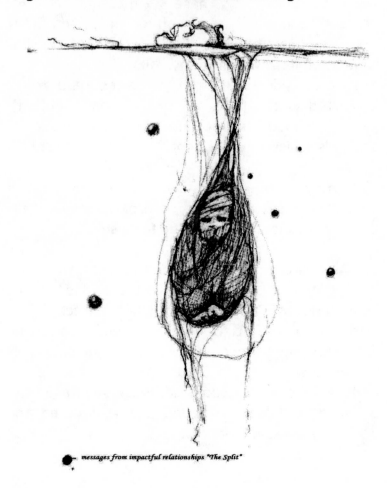

messages from impactful relationships "The Split"

11) Some results include "mental illness," often with traumatic forgetting, chronic emptiness, fear, sadness and confusion, and periodic explosions of self-destructive and other destructive behavior—both impulsive and compulsive—that allow some temporary release of the tension and a glimpse of the true self.

12) The consequences of the continued emptiness and/or repeated destructive behavior keep the true self stifled or submerged. Not living from and as their real self—with a full awareness of their experiences—and with no safe people to talk to about them, the child often feels numb. In order to survive, they may forget, dissociate or otherwise shut out most of their painful experiences (dissociative or traumatic amnesia).

13) The child/person maintains a low sense of self-esteem, remains unhappy, yet wishes for and seeks fulfillment. Compulsions and addictions (and other repetition compulsions) can provide temporary release, but lead to more suffering and ultimately block recovery, fulfillment and serenity.

Recovery

Although they may have had some counseling in the past, will Casey, Cindy, George or Lee Anthony now choose to enter any kind of ongoing counseling, psychotherapy or recovery work? The following sections describe what tends to work best for the healing of most trauma survivors.

14) Recovery and growth involve discovering and gently unearthing the true self (real self, child within, true identity, core being) so that it can exist and express itself in a healthy way, day to day. It also means restructuring the false self or ego to become a more flexible assistant ("positive ego") to the true self. Some other results of working a full recovery program are growth, creativity and increased life energy.

15) Such self-discovery and recovery is usually best accomplished gradually and in the presence of safe, compassionate, skilled and supportive people. Recovery is a cyclical process, and while it has its moments of peace, joy and liberating self-discovery, it is also common to experience periods of confusion and symptoms that appear to be manifestations of "mental illness" and related suffering. Participation in supportive recovery groups teaches the person how to deal with these cycles as they experience how others deal with their emotions, problems and with their growth and accomplishments in the recovery process. With commitment to and active participation in recovery, this healing process may take from three to five years or more.

16) By listening, sharing and reflecting in a safe environment, the trauma survivor begins slowly to remember and confront what happened. They begin to reconstruct the physical, mental and emotional unhealed fragments of memories that

were previously buried deep within their unconscious mind. This crucial period of uncovering and remembering involves a process that evolves slowly over time. It cannot be rushed.

17) During recovery the trauma survivor learns to experience, express and tolerate emotional pain, and by doing so experience their emotional pain's movement and transient nature. This is the opposite of being overwhelmed by and mired in the stagnant pain and numbness of depression, which is commonly accompanied by bothersome anxiety (i.e., fear).

I have written extensively elsewhere about the four main trauma effect healing principles:

1) Discover and practice being our Real Self or Child Within,

2) Identify our ongoing physical, mental-emotional and spiritual needs. Practice getting these needs met with safe and supportive people, over time,

3) Identify, re-experience and grieve the pain of our un-grieved hurts, losses and traumas in the presence of safe and support people, and

4) Identify and work through our core recovery issues which I have described in some detail in *Wisdom to Know the Difference.*

In the next chapter I will describe more about how trauma may have been involved in this case by reviewing what has been reported about how Casey behaved over time and how her family of origin interacted with her.

References

Aggravated child abuse and neglect
www.tennessee.gov/tccy/tnchild/39/39-15-402.htm

Aggravated child abuse and neglect in Florida
www.leg.state.fl.us/Statutes/index.cfm?App_mode=Display_Statute&Search_String=&URL=0800-0899/0827/Sections/0827.03.html

Whitfield CL (2011) *Not Crazy:* You May Not Be Mentally Ill Muse House Press, Atlanta, GA

Whitfield CL (2010) Psychiatric drugs as agents of trauma. *Int J of Risk and Safety in Medicine* 22 (4)195-207

Whitfield CL (2003) *The Truth about Depression*: Choices for Healing. Health Communications, Deerfield Beach, FL

Whitfield CL (2004) *The Truth about Mental Illness*: Choices for Healing. Health Communications, Deerfield Beach, FL, 2004

Whitfield CL (1987) *Healing the Child Within*: Discovery & recovery for adult children of dysfunctional families. Health Communications, Deerfield Beach, FL

Whitfield CL (1990) *A Gift to Myself*: A personal workbook and guide to Healing the Child Within. Health Communications, Deerfield Beach, FL

12 What Core Issues Are Possibly Involved?

What might the primary or core issues have been for Casey Anthony and her family? How might these issues relate to Wendy's description and analysis of this trial?

What issues may have driven Casey to behave in the unhealthy ways that led to the death of her daughter? How may these issues have influenced her and her family's dysfunctional behaviors over time?

You the reader can also ask, "What can *I* learn from this kind of information"? How might I be able to help another child at risk, before it's too late? As a community and nation grieving over Caylee's tragic death and outraged over the lack of justice for an innocent child, what can *we* learn?

In this chapter I address issues that appear relevant to an analysis of dysfunction and distress in the Anthony family and that may have influenced how they treated or mistreated one another and ultimately, indirectly may have resulted in Caylee's death. This is not about blaming anyone. Instead, I will address the four most prominent core issues that I have observed among the relationships between Casey, her parents Cindy and George, and to a lesser extent, her brother Lee.

Core Issue Basics

An issue is any conflict, concern or potential problem, whether conscious or unconscious, that is incomplete for us or needs action or change. A **core** issue is one that comes up repeatedly. We may commonly and unknowingly repeat it so often that it interferes with our day-to-day functioning in our *inner* life and our *outer* life (relationships with our family, friends, others—on or off the job, and elsewhere) that as a result we are too often in conflict, tense and not at peace.

There are at least 15 common core issues in relationships, recovery and life that we can recognize, name and work through. These include:

- Control
- Trust
- Being real
- Feelings
- Low self-esteem (Shame)
- Dependence
- Fear of abandonment
- All-or-none thinking and behaving
- High tolerance for inappropriate behavior
- Over-responsibility for others
- Neglecting my own needs
- Grieving my un-grieved losses
- Difficulty resolving conflict
- Difficulty giving love, and
  Difficulty receiving love

How These Issues May Have Influenced Them

At first it may not be clear which of these core issues is involved for the Anthonys, or any of us. Core issues do not usually present themselves as an "issue." Rather, they present at first as problems in our everyday lives. As problems, concerns, conflicts or patterns arise, we can bring them up with selected safe and supportive people. As we persistently consider and tell our story to safe others it will generally become clear which issue or issues are involved. This knowledge is helpful in our gradually becoming free from confusion, discontent, and unconscious negative life patterns (repetition compulsions or re-enactments).

The Anthonys' Apparent Core Issues

Drawing from what we know of their life history and behavioral profiles, I believe that there are at least four core issues that were particularly pertinent for Casey and her family:

- **Control**,
- **All-or-none** thinking and behaving,
- **High tolerance for inappropriate behavior**, and
- **Low self-esteem**, also known as **shame**.

Casey Marie Anthony was born in Warren, Ohio on March 19, 1986, three years after her brother Lee. Her father George eventually quit his job as a deputy sheriff there and three years later, in 1989, they moved to the Chickasaw Park neighborhood in Orlando where Cindy got a nursing job. They said Casey was a "normal" girl until her senior year at Colonial High School. But is this true? And what did they mean? Normal is a statistical term. It does not mean mentally and emotionally healthy.

While it has been reported that one or more of them may have been in some counseling in the past, their distress appeared to have increased over their unresolved and growing conflicts, especially regarding Caylee's well being.

High Tolerance for Inappropriate Behavior

From my understanding of this case and as a clinician assisting people and families like Casey's for over 30 years, on the surface this is by far the most obvious core issue for Casey and her family.
A prominent example is her family's high tolerance for her repeated lying, which may involve several factors addressed below. The most toxic of Casey's lies involve how she misled her family about Caylee's safety and well-being.

Casey's Repeated Lying

Casey's lies are interwoven among most of her and her family's core issues and may have been but one of several ways that high tolerance for inappropriate behavior showed up in her family. Tolerance for her deceptions may have led to the family's failure to express sufficient concern for Caylee's disappearance for an entire month.

Casey also apparently lied about several important issues, including:

1) Caylee being missing for a full month, 2) where she was taking Caylee repeatedly for "babysitting" *and* that in the middle of the night she was delivering her to unknown locations, 3) her stealing money by borrowing, using stolen checks and her mother's and grandmother's credit cards, 4) her being employed at Universal Studios 5) being on track to graduate from high school and 6) her pregnancy.

There were also the four lies to the police for which she was found guilty at trial.

Lies Can Have Complex Features

Why did so many people in Casey's family let a full month go by before alerting authorities that a child may have been in danger? Cindy did not notify authorities until mid-July, after she retrieved her car and noticed that it smelled like a "dead body." Cindy had repeatedly asked Casey to bring Caylee home and to explain her whereabouts over the month-long period when the child was missing. But she, and apparently George and Lee as well, reluctantly accepted Casey's excuses and irrational explanations for why Caylee was not available.

What about Casey's relationship with the infamous "nanny"? Casey's *own* high tolerance for inappropriate behavior with whoever the nanny was may tell us more about what may have been happening to Caylee over time until her death. As you read in Wendy's earlier chapters, Casey may have been involved in inappropriate activities with Caylee. And Casey was very secretive about these things.

Was Casey making money this way? We know she was not working and had no other apparent income for about two years after she was fired by Kodak. Where did she get money to support herself and her well-publicized "party" lifestyle? Did George and Cindy support her financially? They certainly allowed her to live with them, and they bought food and clothing for Caylee. Did they realize they were supporting a person who may have been involved in nefarious activities, and lying to them about it?

The Anthony family clearly showed a high tolerance for Casey's deceptive and inappropriate behavior. Where families cannot be effective at recognizing signs of trouble, the rest of *us need to pay closer attention to children at risk*, so we can *intervene*. I discuss this potential action in the next chapter.

Needing to be in Control

What do we know about the Anthony family's need for control? Did Casey's parents try to control her too much? Not enough? Did she try to control them? We know that Casey often argued with her parents, and some of their arguments were intense. Intense arguments are usually about control. One of the parties wants something that the other doesn't want to give. Arguments tend to be about who gets what they want or who is in control. Children who grow up in dysfunctional families or are abused tend to have big issues with control.   While Casey's parents probably wanted the best for her, could they have tried to control her to such an extent that she rebelled and did the opposite of their wishes?

As unhealthy as Casey's behavior and life may have been, could she have been trying through her wild lifestyle to assert control over her parents? One piece of evidence that illustrates this attempt at control is Casey's repeated lying. She may have been trying to deceive her parents as well as herself, as a way of justifying her actions and lessening her own emotional pain.

If she were to have been sexually exploiting Caylee in some way, she may have been doing so as a way of lashing out at, thus controlling, her parents in response to their attempts to control Caylee and essentially raise her as their own. Did Casey resent her parents? Did she lie knowing her parents probably did not believe her? Did she believe this would give her control?

This all may have resulted in a vicious cycle of Casey and her parents continually trying to control one another unsuccessfully.

Control is a major issue in lots of relationships. What was control like in your family of origin? Have you ever known anyone with control as an issue? Is Casey's story a reminder of experiences or stories in your life, or in the lives of people you know?

All-or-None Thinking and Behaving

All-or-none thinking and behaving appears to be another core issue in the Anthony family, closely related to the defenses we sometimes employ against the emotional pain of denial and lying. One witness at trial, Melissa England, testified that Casey once bragged to her, "Oh my God, I'm such a good liar."

Another observer said, "A pathological liar like Casey Anthony is simply not created overnight in a vacuum." But while we know Casey lied about some things, do we know for sure whether she is a pathological liar? Was that theme overplayed in this case? Could some of her lies have been to protect herself and her family, as Wendy writes? Were her lies 1) deliberate to cover up some ill deed, 2) related to her or Caylee's safety, 3) the end result of being raised in a dysfunctional family, or 4) some combination of the above?

For some people in troubled or dysfunctional families, lying is an effective coping and survival mechanism. For Casey, it may have been how she managed to deal with what felt like an impossible situation. Some witnesses said that Casey was the center of attention for Lee, Cindy and George. But as Casey got older, her parents may have demanded more than she could deliver. Her ex-fiancé Jesse Grund said, "I saw her abusive household, how her parents treated her with constant negativity. I saw Cindy shame Casey as a failure. They had an adversarial relationship. Casey exaggerated things about her life in order to feel included." To cope with her feelings, Casey may have resorted to telling her parents whatever they wanted to hear because the truth was never good enough for them.

To grow up to be psychologically healthy, children need "two L's": Love and Limits. From what we know it appears that Casey may not have had an adequate amount of either. Cindy and George may not have set appropriate and healthy boundaries and limits for Casey throughout her childhood. Whatever the reasons for Casey's deceptions or lies, if it happened for any of them, child abuse and neglect is often a painful part of family dysfunction that sets up the next generation for more of the same. Over time we may learn more about their family interactions and psychodynamics. But for now, it is enough that a little girl died in circumstances where serious abuse and dysfunction in the child's family appear to have occurred and are at least a part of the story.

Additional Possible Reasons for Casey's Repeated Lies

Most pathological liars tell the truth some of the time. But they lie enough over time *about enough things* to get themselves into repeated trouble with their family, close others, on the job and often with the law. Casey has lost all credibility with most people. But it is worth asking whether she would have developed such a penchant for lying if her parents had set appropriate and healthy boundaries with her throughout her childhood. Cindy and George may have enabled Casey's lies by supporting or ignoring them.

Shame

Given what we know about this case, it is likely that shame has been an important underlying factor for Casey and her family dysfunction.

Different from Guilt

Shame, which is also called low self-esteem, is an uncomfortable or painful feeling that we experience when—consciously or unconsciously—we sense that a part of us is defective, bad, incomplete, inadequate, rotten, phony or a failure. In contrast to *guilt*, where we feel bad from *doing* something wrong, we feel *shame* from believing that we *are* something wrong or bad. Thus guilt seems to be correctable or forgivable, whereas there may seem to be no way out of shame.

In guilt, we have *done* something wrong which we can more easily correct than feelings of shame where we feel, and often believe firmly, that we *are* inherently wrong, and we can see no way to correct ourselves. Often fostered by some organized religions as "original sin," we feel as though we are born defective and bad. From this collective shaming trauma, our false self/ego then maintains the shame. As one patient said, "I have a tape recorder in my head that reminds me of how bad I am."

Where Does Our Shame Come From?

Shame comes from what we do with the negative messages, negative affirmations, beliefs and rules that we hear, see and experience as we grow up in a troubled family and world. We hear and experience abuses from our parents, parent figures, and other people in authority, such as teachers, bosses and clergy. These messages basically tell us that we are somehow not okay. That our feelings, our needs, our true self or child within is inherently flawed and not acceptable.
Shame comes from hearing over and over, messages like, "shame on you!" "You're so bad!" "You're not good enough!" When we hear them often, and from people upon whom we are

dependant and to whom we render ourselves as vulnerable, we believe them as true and unfixable. And so we incorporate or internalize them into our very being and sense of self.

The Shame-Based Family

When people in a dysfunctional family communicate with others from a base or common practice of shame or shaming, it can be described as shame-based interaction. Parents in such a family likely did not have their needs met as children, and usually into adulthood as well. They often use their children to meet many of these unmet needs.

Shame-based families often have a *secret.* This secret may span all kinds of "shameful" events or conditions, from family violence to sexual abuse to alcoholism or another drug addiction to having been in a concentration camp or having a relative who was. The secret can be as subtle as a lost job, a lost promotion or a lost relationship.

Were there Secrets in the Anthony family?

It's hard to know whether any particular family has secrets, but we know that keeping secrets disables all members of the family, whether or not they know the secret. This is because being secretive prevents the expression of questions, concern and feelings (such as fear, anger, shame and guilt). The family thus cannot communicate freely and the true self/child within each family member remains stifled—unable to grow and develop. Certainly, Casey and her family may have had enough secrets to impair their relationships.

Casey's Shame

I quoted Casey's ex-fiancé Jesse Grund above when he said, "I saw Cindy shame Casey as a failure." Given what we know, it is likely that both shame and guilt have been common painful feelings for Casey. *Shame* from:

1) having been repeatedly shamed by people in her family; 2) not graduating from high school; 3) being fired from her job; 4) not being able to find and keep a job thereafter and 5) being an inadequate caregiver to Caylee.

Casey will also likely experience ongoing shame from things that happened *after Caylee disappeared*, including:

1) having been repeatedly arrested (four times within three months); 2) spending three years in jail; 3) losing her daughter to murder; 4) being sued in multiple civil lawsuits; 5) being ordered to serve a year of probation on theft charges; and 6) failing to tell all that she knows about how and why Caylee died.

These are major sources of shame that would be difficult for anyone to bear. Will Casey ever be able to open up to a therapist and talk about the things that led her to make choices that ultimately caused her daughter's death? If she has a serious personality disorder, opening up in a meaningful way is unlikely.

Casey's Guilt

Casey may have experienced *guilt* from: 1) repeatedly lying to people who trusted her and 2) treating her daughter poorly and exposing her to circumstances that led to her death. If Casey has a serious mental condition such as antisocial personality disorder (ASPD—see chapter 16) she may not be able to feel guilt or remorse. Could this be a reason so many observers of this story and trial have been so enraged at Casey? Can we understand when someone like this seems to lack the capacity to feel these basic human emotions?

Other Core Issues

Other core issues in the Anthony family appear to include things like *difficulty trusting* and *difficulty giving and receiving love*. For example, when Cindy stepped down from witness stand after testifying at the murder trial, she said silently to Casey, "I love you." The camera then showed Casey's reaction to her mother's expression of love. Casey responded by looking away with distain.

PTSD and Core Issues

Casey and her family may well have post-traumatic stress disorder (PTSD), which can exaggerate and trigger core issues. It appeared during the trial that they were all undergoing repeated and serious stressors and experienced much distress. Look at Table 12.1 below and see if you can identify stressors that Casey and her family may have been experiencing. This table lists only a few examples of stressors.

I would estimate that *their* stress and distress levels were in the range of moderate to extreme and at times possibly catastrophic. It is no surprise that their dysfunction and pain during the past six years has increased for all of them.

As parents and grandparents many of us have compassion for all in the Anthony family and their increased emotional pain and suffering. Their burden has become a collective lesson for all of us to learn more about what children need.

These core issues come up repeatedly for trauma survivors. I have described some of them and their dynamics as they appear to have been involved in the lives of Casey Anthony and her closest family members.

Table 12.1 Severity Rating of Psychosocial Stressors (from DSM-3)

Severity: Child/Adolescent Examples	Adult Examples
1. **None** No apparent psychological stressor	No apparent psychological stressor
2. **Minimal** Vacation with family	Minor violation of the law; small bank loan
3. **Mild** Change in schoolteacher; new school year	Argument with neighbor; change in work hours
4. **Moderate** Chronic parental fighting; change to new school; illness of close relative; sibling birth	New career; death of close friend; pregnancy
5. **Severe** Death of peer; divorce of parents; arrest; hospitalization; persistent separation; and harsh parental discipline	Serious illness in self or family; major financial loss; marital separation birth of child and harsh parental discipline
6. **Extreme** Death of parent or sibling; repeated physical or sexual abuse	Death of close relative; divorce
7. **Catastrophic** Multiple family deaths	Devastating natural disaster; concentration camp experience

(My recent book *Not Crazy* has more on PTSD.)

In the next chapter I will describe ways that we can help to protect all children from child abuse and neglect.

References

johnhgohde.wordpress.com/2009/01/12/casey-anthony-family-dynamics/ Pathological lying reference accessed online 29 Aug 2011

Grund J (2011) interviewed on Dr Drew HLN TV, 23 July

Casey's lies justice4caylee.forumotion.net/t13538-casey-anthony-trial-oh-my-god-i-m-such-a-good-liar-casey-told-witness-os   accessed online 29 Aug 2011

Jail letters (2011) wftv.com/pdf/23069597/detail.html accessed online 29 Aug

Ablow K foxnewsinsider.com/2011/07/18/dr-keith-ablow-casey-anthony-needs-the-most-extraordinary-psychotherapy-you-can-imagine/
accessed online 29 Aug 2011

OCSO files investigation.discovery.com/blogs/criminal-report/casey_anthony_full_coverage/files/casey_anthony_documents03.pdf accessed online 29 Aug 2011

Lehman J (2011) Empowering Parents program ratings.thetotaltransformation.com/index4.php?dsource=GoogleB3&gclid=CLXR87fB26oCFUFo4Aod2HyP7g

Whitfield CL (2012) *Wisdom to Know the Difference: Core issues in relationships, recovery and life.* Muse House Press, Atlanta

Whitfield CL (1993) *Boundaries and Relationships: Knowing, Protecting and Enjoying the Self.* Health Communications, Deerfield Beach, FL

Anthony C & G (2011) Appearances on 3-part interview TV series with Dr Phil, September 13, 14, 19

Grace N (2011) on HLN Commentaries by guest experts, July through end September

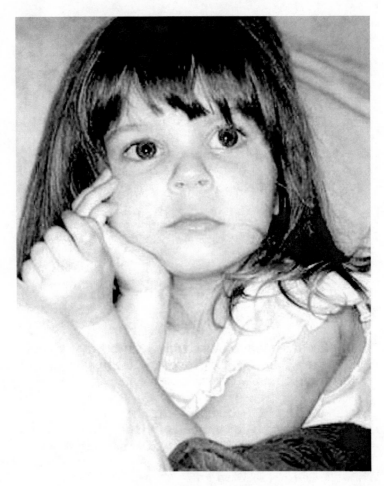

Caylee Marie Anthony

13   Prevention

How Can We Prevent Similar Deaths and What Are The Warning Signs?

As you learned from reading Wendy's chapters, much happened in this case that has *not* been reported in the mainstream media. In this chapter I will continue to describe this information from the perspective of prevention. Given what we know about child abuse and neglect from more than 50 years of research, *how can we prevent similar deaths* in the future?

Childhood Deaths in Perspective

Children die every day from child abuse and neglect, most of which goes undetected and unreported. In a recent report, researchers reveal startling data, as shown in Table 13.1.

Five abused children die *each day* in the United States, which is *twice* the *total* of the five other causes of death *for all ages*.[1] These figures are rarely discussed in the media and are seldom reported in the research and clinical literature or in

---

1 These data are from the report *We Can Do Better*: Child Abuse and Neglect Deaths in America, by Every Child *matters* Education fund, Washington, DC, available at:

www.childdeathreview.org/Promo?CAN_Report.pdf

Table 13.1 Yearly Child Abuse and Neglect Fatalities vs. Other Causes of Death July 2007- June 2008

Cause of death	Most recent data
U.S. soldiers killed in Iraq & Afghanistan in 2009	479
H1N1 pediatric deaths 2009	281
Food borne illnesses 2009	74
Toyota accelerator malfunction 2000 – 2010	34
Coal mining accidents 2009	33
Total other causes of death	901
Total child abuse & neglect fatalities	1,740

official publications from county, state or federal governments.

Imagine five children dying every day in circumstances related to the death of Caylee Anthony.

Prevention Summary

I believe there are six main actions that we can take to help prevent future deaths from child abuse and neglect.

1) Help ourselves and others to understand what childhood trauma is, and how it causes detrimental effects across generations;

2) Stop abusing and neglecting children;

3) Teach parents healthy skills, including how to set boundaries and limits;

4) Support the responsible use of birth control, for males and females;

5) Encourage parents of unwanted children to give them up for adoption;

6) Advocate for aggressive community involvement in at-risk families.

I will address each of these ideas in turn.

> **1. Help ourselves and others to understand what childhood trauma is, and how it causes detrimental effects across generations.**

Over the last several decades researchers and clinicians have learned several important things about child abuse and neglect that bear at least some connection to this distressing and tragic case. I already described in chapter 11 what it is and how it happens. Here is a short summary of what we know about child abuse and neglect:

a) Child abuse and neglect cause traumatic effects that hurt the child so much that the child loses their full awareness of who they are, their Real Self, which, as I described above in chapter 11, is also called the Child Within. Their Real Self goes into hiding (Figure 11.1, above).

To survive in a troubled and painful family, unconsciously they let their false self or ego run their life. Of course, a false self is not capable of running anyone's life in a healthy way for very long.

b) Child abuse and neglect cause further traumatic effects that can leave the child's brain, nervous system and body damaged and less able to live a healthy life. Despite common claims to the contrary, *many brain abnormalities are not inherited,* but are *caused by trauma*.

c) These effects commonly manifest as one variant or another of post-traumatic stress disorder (PTSD) and a list of other detrimental or life-deflating effects. Some of these negative results include subsequent unhealthy parenting such that the original child abuse and neglect brings about in the next generation—*still more* unhealthy parenting of the original parents' grandchildren.

d) In this *vicious cycle*, abuse and neglect begets children who then tend to grow up to abuse and neglect their own children, and so on. Often, countless others are affected as well, such as spouses and close friends and family.

e) Other negative effects include "mental illness" (including personality *disorders* and dysfunctional personality *traits*), promiscuity, unplanned teen pregnancy, unhealthy parenting, eating disorders, addictions and compulsions, criminal behavior, and as mentioned above, PTSD (Figure 13.1).

Consider how many of these serious problems were or may have been parts of Casey Anthony's life.

Study this above list and look at figure 13.1 for a minute.

How many of these serious problems do you sense that Casey Anthony had?

Where do you guess they came from?   How may they have developed?

Figure 13.1 The Vicious Cycle of Child Abuse & Neglect Produces Serious Problems

Key: CA/N = Child Abuse & Neglect, PTSD = Post-traumatic Stress Disorder

f) A final effect of unhealthy parenting and child abuse and neglect in the Casey Anthony situation is criminal behavior. This vicious cycle of child abuse and neglect often produces criminal behavior that may include: pathological lying and perjury, fraud, extortion and blackmail, robbery, illegal drug dealing, driving under the influence of alcohol or other drugs, child abuse and neglect, child molesting, domestic and other physical violence, sexual assault, homicide and child pornography. (Figure 13.2).

Study this list and Figure 13.2 for a minute. Which of these ten criminal behaviors do you sense that Casey may have manifested?

Figure 13.2 The Vicious Cycle of Child Abuse & Neglect Produces Criminal Behavior

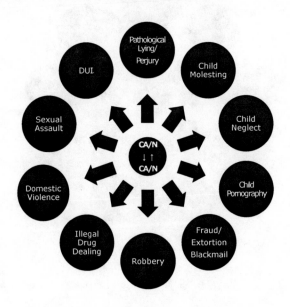

2. Stop abusing and neglecting children

This one seems simple. After learning what child abuse and neglect are, which I describe in chapter 12 above, we should simply stop doing them. But it is not easy to stop a cycle of behavior produced by the actions of past generations. Nevertheless, we all can openly *commit* to not doing any of these abusive actions with our children.

An important part of healthy parenting is knowing how and when to discipline the child by setting limits on their misbehavior. We help the child, ourself and others around us by giving the child healthy guidance and unconditional love, while setting appropriate limits when necessary.

3. Teach parents healthy parenting including how to set boundaries & limits

This is not easy, for several reasons. We usually learn about parenting by watching how our own parents treat us. Parents model to their kids how to do all kinds of things, including parenting. Few of us learn by taking a course. To get a driver's license, we have to have some amount of training and pass a test. But having a child requires no skill whatsoever. Here is where our educational system can make a difference.

If we were actually taught in school about children's physical, psychological and spiritual needs, all parents would have better information to help them choose whether to raise a child or—if they believed they could not handle it—release the child for adoption. Parenting education could also help all children learn to be good parents, no matter what they are learning at home.

Any parent who chooses not put a child up for adoption should be offered an opportunity to learn healthy parenting skills. If grandparents become involved in raising their children's children, they should also be entitled to receive skills assistance. Such a program for grandparents is already in place in states like Georgia.

Quality education for single parents and grandparents may be part of a solution to our huge welfare conundrum which would also contribute to saving our children from abuse and neglect.

4. Support the responsible use of birth control, for males and females

Facts

• The unplanned child's *single* mother and her family—usually the parents—*will be* the child's *caretakers* for *at least the next 20 years* of the child's life.

• The biological father usually *will not* be much or any of a caretaker, if he's involved at all.

Ideas

• Help teenagers understand the risks to their lives and futures. Many single mothers have a baby because their family didn't give them enough love. Teach teens that having a baby will not give them the love that they never had.

• Being a single parent is a *big disadvantage* for any girl or woman. Children are needy, demanding and draining of the mother's time, energy, and finances. Teach teens not to do this to themselves and the baby. And biological fathers are often forced by courts to pay child support for 18 years. It is expensive and most teens can't afford to raise a child.

• Someone—parents or other appropriate parent figures—should teach young people about the availability and proper use of birth control *before* they start having sex.

Unplanned Teen Pregnancy

Another way to prevent child abuse and neglect is to address unplanned teen pregnancies. About half of all births today in the United States are from unplanned or unwanted pregnancies involving single mothers. It is significant that a majority of child neglect and related problems occur to children being raised in these single parent families.

Eighty-five percent of mothers who *kill their children through neglect* are *single parents*.

It appears that child neglect and related problems may be causally related to single motherhood status, especially if the biological father takes no responsibility in caring for the child.

Casey Anthony is reported to have told her close friend, Kiomarie Cruz, early on in her pregnancy that she was indeed pregnant. Kiomarie asked if she would let her adopt her baby because a doctor had told her that she couldn't have her own. Casey agreed at first, but she later said Cindy wouldn't allow it. This refusal to release Caylee for adoption may have cost Casey, her family and society untold grief—and it may have cost Caylee her life. Studies show that adopted children tend to do better in life than non-adopted, as I explain below.

5. Encourage parents of unwanted Children to give them up for adoption

Various studies have shown that children raised by single mothers comprise about 70% of juvenile murderers, delinquents, teen-age mothers, drug abusers, drop outs, suicides and runaways. By contrast, adopted kids on average turn out better than even biological kids raised in two-parent families. There aren't a lot of studies of children who do well because we don't tend to study the behavior of kids who do well.

In one study, adopted teenagers were found to have greater empathy, higher self esteem and more close friends than non-adopted teenagers in public schools, and were less likely to engage in high risk behaviors, such as stealing and excessive drinking. They scored higher than the control group on 16 indicators of well-being. Most adopted teens rarely thought about the fact that they were adopted.

Between 1979 and 2003, we went from about 600,000 babies being born to single mothers, with about a quarter of them put up for adoption, to 1.5 million illegitimate births with fewer than 1 percent of them (14,000) given up for adoption.

6. Advocate for aggressive community involvement in at-risk families

Knowing all these things about child abuse, what can we do differently to better protect children: 1) within our family, 2) in our local communities, and 3) in our nation as a whole?

1) Within our family – When we see ourselves or family members engaged in the abuse or neglect of a child, depending on the severity and acuteness of the mistreatment, we should intervene in a polite but firm or assertive manner and make it known that we disapprove, and that the behavior must stop. We then need to monitor and follow through with our goal of zero tolerance for abuse and neglect by asking questions, and staying involved in the child's life. Too often, observing abuse makes people uncomfortable, so they stop visiting or socializing with the abusive adults. This can put a victimized child at greater risk of injury.

2) In our local communities – Here it may be more difficult for us to identify child abuse and intervene as easily as we can with our families. But if we express our concerns in a non-threatening manner, we can at least point out that we object and that we care about children's well-being. If we see a parent abuse a child in a food market or public facility, how can we intervene appropriately? It may depend on the community, and the circumstances, but we won't know whether intervening will help unless we try, and we know that doing nothing may expose a child to harm. Some countries have supported this philosophy for decades, with success. We could at least give it a try.

3) In our nation as a whole – If we know of abuse and neglect and have no other recourse to prevent it, we can contact our local child protective services agency and report what we have observed in the hope they will intervene.

Reference

Single parent data (accessed 30 August, 2011) albanymediabias.blogspot.com/2011/07/your-random-saturday_09.html

Part Three: Grieving and Making Meaning

by Barbara Whitfield, RT

14   How Can We Accept the Unacceptable?

For the past three years, some in our media have focused an extraordinary amount of attention on the disappearance and death of only one child—Caylee Anthony. We have been repeatedly reminded of extremely painful and unbelievable facts about her gruesome death. Caylee's face on the screen, descriptions and pictures of her remains, Casey's party pictures, and more —reminding us every day of all the missing or murdered children who literally slip through the cracks. How can this happen? My head spins with the pain of this child's plight. My heart keeps telling me that children should be protected, not harmed. "Children," after all, "are our future." As you've read throughout this book, five abused children die *every day* in this country.

Wendy Murphy has described the legal aspects of this tragic story of child abuse and neglect and has raised some crucial questions about what may be underlying this problematic and ongoing case. Charles Whitfield summarized important aspects of

165

the nature of child abuse and neglect and addressed core issues in this case and ways that we as individuals and communities can prevent this kind of thing from happening again.

In this chapter and the next, I will address how we can begin to move through the feelings that this tragedy evoked in us as individuals, and as a nation. We have suffered as observers through this ordeal, and we need some kind of closure, which is especially difficult in the aftermath of a not guilty verdict. We feel a loss for the child, not only because of her death but also because justice was not served. We need to make some kind of meaning in a case that has left us helpless, frustrated, angry and profoundly sad. One opportunity may be that we can find meaning in our collective grieving.

Depression vs. Sadness and Grieving

As we individually try to make sense of this atrocity, many of us may feel that we are sinking into "depression." As a thanatologist (one who studies death and dying) and grief counselor I can explain the significant difference between being depressed and being sad and grieving.

When we grieve, sadness overtakes us and rules our life for a while. But there is hope and things do change. Eventually we move through sadness and make meaning out of loss. Moving through this process of grieving takes on a bittersweet feeling.

When we are depressed, we are numb and there is no movement. Society used to make room for the grieving process. We had periods of time where we were supported on many levels, and could take time for healing. Now, grieving has been reduced to a few days off work and then back to business as usual. Rather than honor healthy grieving, our society has convinced us that a "quick fix" will do the trick and that prescription drugs will relieve our pain. But drugs only put our grief work on "hold" where it will remain until we stop the drugs and allow ourselves to feel our pain. It takes courage to face our losses, but from that process of embracing our feelings, we can come to a new way of being that incorporates our experience of having grieved. We grow. In my experiences helping others grieve, and in my own grieving process, I have witnessed over and over again that the one who has left us or died gives us the gift of growing more of ourselves through the grieving process.

Accepting the Unacceptable

Finding a way to process our own feelings, accepting the painful reality of Caylee's untimely and horrific death is another way we can find meaning in this tragedy. When we judge information that is unfair, terrible or even devastating, we usually find the experience too difficult to accept, so we transfer our feelings about the situation into what we believe about the justice system and the world. We need to make sense of things, but we only have our own inner life by which to process information. When things don't "fit," as in Caylee's case, we tend to fill in the blanks with what we do know. The problem is, this processing experience caused most of us to turn an unintentional blind eye to the ugly truth.

At the same time, we feel desperate for answers that explain all that we do know about how and why Caylee died. Did this poor baby have any comfort in her last moments? What kind of person could kill a child? Did she suffer before she died? Our anger and frustration at not knowing can become a driving force in our lives, removing our ability ever to accept the unacceptable and move on.

A Letter to all of Us about Caylee's Death

The untimely, brutal murder of Caylee Anthony is a terrible experience that we face together as a nation. It requires us to accept the unacceptable. We wonder, "Why do children die?" I once wrote a story of a couple that knew their baby was going to die at birth from birth defects. Instead of running from the situation, they faced it head on and dealt with their sadness directly. When the baby was born, the parents cradled and loved their baby for the few minutes while the child was alive. Then they honored him with a memorial service where they talked about how they will always carry their precious child's soul in their hearts. I finished the story by including an amazing letter by a former Harvard psychology professor who has become a spiritual teacher to many of us. When he was at Harvard, he was known as Richard Alpert PhD. After years of meditation and study in the East, he returned to the United States to write and teach as Ram Dass.

A number of years ago, Ram Dass responded to the distraught parents of a child who had just died in a tragic murder that was similar to Caylee's. His response to them fits here and may well assist us as we consider how we feel about Caylee's story. I include it below, changing the murdered child's name to Caylee and editing it just enough to change the circumstances so that this letter can help each of us address our emotional torment over the horrendous death of Caylee Anthony:

Dear fellow grievers, Caylee finished her work on earth, and left the stage in a manner that leaves those of us left behind with a cry of agony in our hearts, as the fragile thread of our faith is dealt with so violently. Is anyone strong enough to stay conscious through such teaching as we are receiving? Probably very few, and even they would only have a whisper of equanimity and peace amidst the screaming trumpets of their rage, grief, horror and desolation.

I can't assuage your pain with any words, nor should I. For your pain is Caylee's legacy to all of us. Not that she or I would inflict such pain by choice, but there it is. And it must burn its purifying way to completion. For something in us dies when we bear the unbearable, and it is only in that dark night of the Soul that we are prepared to see as God sees, and to love as God loves.

Now is the time to let our grief find expression. No false strength. Now is the time to sit quietly and speak to Caylee, and thank her for being with us these few years, and encourage her to go on with whatever her work is, knowing that you will grow in compassion and wisdom from this experience.

In my heart, I know that we will all meet again and again, and recognize the many ways in which we have known each other. And when we meet we will know, in a flash, what now it is not given to us to know: Why this had to be the way it was.

Our rational minds can never understand what has happened, but our hearts—if we can keep them open to God—will find their own intuitive way. Caylee came through to do her work on earth, which includes her manner of death. Now her Soul is free, and the love that we all can share with her is invulnerable to the winds of changing time and space. In that deep love, include me.
In love,
Ram Dass

References

Whitfield B (2010) *The Natural Soul:* Unity with the Spiritual Energy that Connects Us. Muse House Press, Atlanta, GA

Whitfield B (1998) *Final Passage*: Sharing the Journey as this life ends. Health Communications, Inc. Deerfield Beach, FL

Ram Dass talks ramdasstapes.org/articles_final.htm

15 How Can We Make Meaning out of This Atrocity?

As you read this chapter, you may wonder how this information applies to the Casey Anthony case. Bear with me while I describe academic research and my own experience through which I will bring together all this seemingly unrelated material and give us a different and new hope for justice for Caylee, and countless other abused children.

As a researcher and author of near-death studies for more than 35 years, and as a person who had my own near-death experience (NDE), I have been engaged in a powerful *Life Review* that has percolated for decades. This is my first opportunity, and maybe even the first time in the literature that someone is applying the consequences of a *Life Review* to a murder case to show how justice can prevail in the end.

Most of us have experienced unacceptable events in our lives; events so traumatic, difficult and painful that we cannot possibly imagine how or why they happened. Add to that, the fact that this tragic case is filled with secrets, sealed photographs of Caylee and files the court has not released to the public. The absurd juxtapositions of truth and drama leave us feeling totally confused. Yet, even when we cannot make sense of things, it is possible to find clarity and truth. The following is a first person account of a *Life Review* during an NDE that demonstrates how one can cut through confusion and find clarity and truth:

"... *It was like watching my life from start to finish on an editing machine stuck in fast forward. The review took me from my conception which felt like the blackness I experienced after my out of body experience, through my childhood, to adolescence, into my teens, and through my near death experience over again. I saw my life. I re-lived my life. I felt everything I ever felt before. When I say 'everything,' I mean every cut, pain, emotion and sense associated with that particular time in my life. At the same time, I saw the effects of my life on the people around me.... I felt all that they felt and, through this, I understood the repercussions of everything I did, be it good or bad. This Life Review was the most beautiful thing I had ever seen. And at the same time, the most horrifying thing I was ever to experience."*

—Neev, student, reporting to Professor
Kenneth Ring from *Lessons from the Light*

What have we learned from the research on NDEs?

For six years I was research assistant to Bruce Greyson, MD at the University of Connecticut Medical School examining the after-effects of NDEs.

The only comfort I found during the Casey Anthony Trial as I kept thinking about how and why Caylee died, is what my colleagues and I have heard over and over again in our interviews with near-death experiencers: *no one dies alone*. We learned this from hundreds, if not thousands, of interviews.

My own NDE demonstrates this same principle. I was suspended in a Stryker frame circle bed after spinal surgery. A few days after the operation, I started to die. I had been an atheist until that moment, never thinking that there was an existence after death. Yet my grandmother, who had been dead for 14 years, was there somehow and she immediately comforted me as we moved through a tunnel.

Many children who report NDEs have told me about a beautiful lady with long blond hair who met them immediately, took their hand and walked with them. In several books on childhood NDEs, similar experiences are described that involve children being met by someone as they near death. In Todd Burpo's *Heaven is for Real*, he tells the story of his

3 year-old son's experience after a burst appendix. (Also see the writings of pediatrician Melvin Morse.)

Research into near-death experiences gives me a great deal of hope that Caylee had love all around her when she died. Even children who suffer trauma that does not cause a near-death event have told me about leaving their bodies during the trauma and watching from above, sometimes then seeing other realities and being surrounded by love. This is reported from adults as well, during traumatic events, or even in anticipation of a trauma that doesn't happen. These so-called "out-of-body" experiences can be a natural reaction under extreme stress. If Caylee was abused during this lifetime, she may have had many such experiences. They would have helped her cope by, in a sense, taking her away from unimaginable horror. I hope that however she managed abuse during her short life, she was out of her body when she was murdered, and was surrounded by love at the moment of her death.

Can Justice and Resolution Ever be Achieved?

A week after my first NDE, I again left my body in the circle bed and had what we call the *Life Review*. For years I couldn't find words to describe what I went through, but I was held by an incredibly loving Energy that I can only call "God." My *Life Review* enabled me to experience a linear sequence of my life, reminding me that I had been abused and neglected as a child. I saw and *felt* so many things about my life, all over again. This made me realize that we are all connected to each other and don't end at our skin. It showed me that we continue to exist after our "death." Our body may die but there is a part of us that continues. I learned that we are all connected in this dance of life and everything we do affects others, now and forever. The most profound and practical part of this *Life Review* was that I could see I was becoming like my mother with my own children. She had taught me well just as her family had taught her. And I knew I needed to change so that my children would not have to go through what I did. It was time to break the links to an intergenerational chain of abuse and neglect. *This may have occurred in Casey's family from her parents to herself and then to Caylee – across three generations.* I knew that the first thing I needed to learn was how to listen. In my family I saw that everyone manipulated and overpowered to control each other. No one listened. Everyone was talking at each other but not listening. *Did any of these dynamics happen with Casey and her family?*

I hope that one day soon, Casey Anthony will have a *Life Review* too. It could be a life-changing event for her that not only enables Casey to tell the whole truth about how Caylee lived and died, but also frees her to know *what it feels like* to feel *true love* between a *mother* and her *child*.

Social Psychologist Kenneth Ring PhD calls the *Life Review* "The Cosmic Equalizer." He argues that no one else sits in judgment of us. We watch ourselves, and are responsible for everything in all the scenes of our lives – and we don't just feel our own feelings, we feel the feelings of others who are affected because of our actions.

NDE survivor Dannion Brinkley gives us this summary of his Life Review:

"When you have a panoramic Life Review, you literally re-live your life ... and you watch your life from a second person's point of view...When I finished the Life Review, I arrived at a point of reflection in which I was able to look back ... and I was ashamed. I realized I had led a very selfish life, rarely reaching out to help anyone ... my life had been for me and me alone. I hadn't given a damn about my fellow humans."

Brinkley has gone on to change his life by working to help further the causes of hospice. Those who know him say he has completely changed.

Dr. Greyson says: "... people who were in very punitive or violent professions can be totally shaken up by the NDE and not be able to go back to their lives as they were before. There were a lot of people who had NDEs in Vietnam, who had been career military people. They just couldn't go back to it ... Having a near-death-experience is a profound event, from which most people come back changed. Criminals return ready to serve others."

From my own *Life Review*, and from interviews with hundreds of other near-death experiencers, I have no doubt that justice will be served when the person or persons who did kill Caylee find a way to see and to feel everything they were responsible for in the abuse, neglect and atrocious death of a defenseless child.

Are we waking up in this Collective *Life Review*?

Our individual, public and collective reactions to the atrocity of this case have triggered and roused within us an awareness of the evil that each of us allows to happen when we turn our backs on child abuse and neglect. In a sense this case is taking us through a kind of *Life Review* and is waking us up to the need to name *and then prevent* such pain and damage from happening ever again to any other child. *Could this be the gift that Caylee's short little life has given us?*

Could Casey's apparent uncaring character mirror our own cavalier attitude toward child abuse and neglect? Have we been fearful of confronting child abuse head on because of fear that the problem is too large, or that we might uncover ugly things about our friends and neighbors? But in this big story, because of one little girl, we have somehow become unafraid. This is a gift. The outcry on behalf of a single child has been tremendous. The challenge now is to keep the momentum going, in a collective fight for the whole truth about why Caylee died, and to ensure that no other child suffers a similar fate ever again.

References

Burpo T (2010) *Heaven is for Real* Thomas Nelson Publisher, Nashville TN

Holden J, Greyson B, James D (2009) *Handbook of Near-Death Experiences.* Praeger Publishers Santa Barbara, CA

Morse M (1990) *Closer to the Light: Learning from the Near-Death Experiences of Children*. Random House, New York, NY

Ring K (1998) *Lessons from the Light*. Plenum Press Insight, New York & London

(Whitfield) Harris Barbara (1990) *Full Circle* Simon and Schuster, NY, NY

Whitfield B (1995) *Spiritual Awakenings: Insights of the Near-Death Experience and other doorways to our Soul.* Health Communications, Inc. Deerfield Beach, FL

Whitfield B (2011) *Victim to Survivor and Thriver: Carole's Story* Muse House Press, Atlanta GA

Part Four: The Future

16 What's Next For Casey, Her Family and the Rest of Us?

by Wendy Murphy JD, Charles Whitfield MD, and Barbara Whitfield RT

Her Challenges

Casey will need to make a living, not to mention deal with several lawsuits, a $70,000 tax lien and a new $217,449 judge's order to reimburse law enforcement against her, while she figures out the next steps in her life.

She could also face more criminal charges, depending on what's hidden in the sealed files, and what the FBI decides to do with its investigation.

Assuming the sealed evidence in this case relates to prostitution and/or child pornography, recall that in earlier chapters we discussed two key reasons the information would have been placed under seal and excluded from trial. One is that the information was never directly connected to Caylee's murder. If highly prejudicial information is not strongly related to proof of the crime, which is to say the evidence does not help to prove or disprove guilt, the court would be compelled to exclude such information as unduly prejudicial without sufficient probative force.

Remember that Casey was offered immunity early on in this case. She reportedly refused a deal which would have required her to tell what she knew about the involvement of others in Caylee's disappearance. Even if cops had already found evidence of child porn, they would have been unable to tie the porn to Caylee's disappearance in the absence of someone explaining the connection. Without it, the evidence would add nothing to the state's proof of murder. The second reason such information would have been "sealed" is that the feds are involved in investigating issues related to the sealed evidence and they want to be able to proceed on those charges against Casey, and/or others, in federal court. If the evidence had been allowed in during the murder trial, Casey's acquittal may have precluded retrial on the porn charges under double jeopardy principles.

Double jeopardy means a person cannot be tried for the same crime twice, but the concept is not limited to retrial on the same *charges.* It also forbids retrial on the same *facts*. Under the Supreme Court's "same facts" Blockburger test, if the state offered evidence of Casey Anthony's involvement with prostitution or child pornography, those facts may not have been admissible against her in a subsequent prosecution. We know that there was a collateral federal investigation going on during the state's investigation of Caylee's murder.

Although some of the interviews of witnesses and details of the investigation are being withheld from public view at the moment, there are references to the feds being involved and witnesses being interviewed by the FBI regarding matters not yet disclosed.

We know that the *federal* investigation, at least to some extent, is not related to the murder case against Casey Anthony because if it were, all FBI interviews would have been released to the public by now. It happens sometimes, in kidnapping cases, that both federal and state officials get involved in taking witness statements. But if charges are brought in state court, as was the case here, all federal investigation files become part of the state prosecution's file. Yet, not all of the federal evidence has been released. For example, we know that Lee Anthony was interviewed by both FBI and state law enforcement officials, but only the statements he gave to state officials have been released. Why?

Again, some of the federal evidence was sealed to protect Casey's due process rights at trial. But now that that she's been acquitted, the truth should be told and all files should be released.

That said, there's a good chance public demand for full disclosure of FBI files and the sealed information in the state's case will not succeed because officials will claim the case is still "pending," notwithstanding the not guilty verdict. What could still be "pending" you wonder? One argument is that the federal investigation is not yet over. In the state case, the more likely claim will be related to the fact that Casey's attorneys recently filed an appeal from her convictions for lying to police. By filing an appeal, they can now argue that the court's order "sealing" certain evidence must remain in effect until all appellate proceedings are resolved. This could take years and should raise even more public suspicion as to whether the appeal is a smokescreen. This is because, as was made clear to the prosecutor's office when they asserted that excuse as a reason to refuse to release sealed photographs of Caylee and certain search warrants after the verdict, even a rookie law student can see that an appeal on the lying charges is an exercise in futility.

Casey cannot possibly win a reversal of her convictions for lying because she *admitted* to lying, she's already served the maximum punishment on each count and the defense did not even rebut the charges at trial or mention them during closing argument. The only possible purpose of an appeal is to erect an excuse to further thwart the public's right to know the truth about the "sealed" evidence, and ultimately, what really happened to little Caylee.

The Orlando Sentinel filed a Motion in the case after the verdict, seeking release of some sealed files, but they explicitly did not seek the release of sealed photos of Caylee, or search warrants for the various computers that may have contained child pornography. Why not? Why would a newspaper file a request asking for release of only *certain* information but not *all* sealed files? And why are some reporters claiming there are no sealed photographs of Caylee when the evidence revealed in this book clearly shows otherwise?

The harder that people try to keep the sealed files secret, the more determined we all have to be in the fight to make sure that one day, the truth will be told.

Casey's Personal Healing

Given what we know about Casey, especially if she has a personality disorder, it is unlikely—short of very hard work on her inner life and outer behavior over a long period of time—that she will be able to make good use of psychotherapy. We know that psychiatric drugs have little or no effect in improving the life of a person with a personality disorder. We also know that with most "mental illness" these drugs too often make people worse, not better. Casey may have a personality disorder of some type, including the possibility of borderline personality, antisocial personality, or a mixed personality disorder, and may have dissociative features. The term "personality" disorder is somewhat of a misnomer because it may be more correct to say she suffers from a *behavior* disorder, or a *moral* and *ethical* behavior disorder.

The Diagnostic Manual for mental health disorders lists the following criteria for a diagnosis of antisocial personality disorder (ASPD). As you read over these criteria, put a check mark next to each one that fits with Casey's history as you know it. Then draw your own conclusions.

The *Diagnostic and Statistical Manual of Mental Disorders* fourth edition, DSM IV-TR, a widely used manual for diagnosing "mental disorders," defines ASPD (code 301.7 in Axis II "Cluster B") as:

A) There is a pervasive pattern of disregard for and violation of the rights of others occurring since age 15 years, as indicated by *three or more* of the following:

1) failure to conform to social norms with respect to lawful behaviors as indicated by repeatedly performing acts that are grounds for arrest;
2) deception, as indicated by repeatedly lying, use of aliases, or conning others for personal profit or pleasure;
3) impulsiveness or failure to plan ahead;
4) irritability and aggressiveness, as indicated by repeated physical fights or assaults;
5) reckless disregard for safety of self or others;

6) consistent irresponsibility, as indicated by repeated failure to sustain consistent work behavior or honor financial obligations;
7) lack of remorse, as indicated by being indifferent to or rationalizing having hurt, mistreated, or stolen from another.

B) At least 18 years-old.
C) There is evidence of conduct disorder with onset before age 15 years.
D) The occurrence of antisocial behavior is not exclusively during the course of schizophrenia or a manic episode.

The DSM adds a note about children: "Children often develop antisocial personality disorder as a result of *environmental* (childhood trauma) as well as genetic influence. The prevalence of this disorder is 3% in men and 1% in women."

Staying Out of Trouble

Will Casey be able to stay out of trouble? Given what we know about her history over the past few years, it seems unlikely, and the stress of being under society's microscope for the rest of her life may be difficult for Casey to manage. OJ Simpson ended up in trouble with the law after his acquittal on murder charges, and while it took a few years before his behavior escalated to crime, again, he is now serving a long prison sentence because he could not stay out of trouble. Casey may endure a similar fate—a kind of existential hell from which she may likely never recover. In fact, she may be emboldened by the not guilty verdict, leading her to choose a path that will land her back behind bars even faster than the time it took for OJ Simpson to finally meet his destiny.

Another Child?

Will Casey have another child? Some reports say she plans to have more children. If this is true, the world will be watching her behavior with that child very carefully, as will child protective services and law enforcement officials in whatever state she finds herself at the moment she gives birth.

Her Safety and Survival

Will there continue to be threats against Casey's life? The outrage produced by this trial leaves many more questions than answers about how long Casey will remain in the public eye and how long the public's anger toward her will be sustained. Her lawyer claims she has been threatened, and she was recently voted "The Most Hated Person" in America. Thus far, however, she has suffered no physical retaliation from an angry public.

Her Family

What will happen to Casey's family? What is next for them? It has been reported that Cindy wanted Casey to come home and George did not. If so, how will they handle this tension as they go about their daily lives? What will happen at her brother

Lee Anthony's upcoming wedding? Will Casey attend? Dysfunctional families have trouble managing ordinary stress. The Anthonys will find it difficult to navigate life with the added burdens of extraordinary pressure that come with a trial of such magnitude and high emotion. Hopefully, the Anthonys, with or without Casey in their lives, will seek professional help for their ongoing issues and distress. Whether it makes a difference remains to be seen.

What about Us?

And what about us? What about the stress that this story and trial has produced in the public's eyes and hearts? Much of this book addresses ways of handling our feelings. It won't be easy, and not everyone benefits from the same healing strategies. It is important to continue to talk about the case, and to share our thoughts not only with each other, but also with those people in our lives who care for children.

We also have a duty to continue to talk to law enforcement, court officials, prosecutors and media professionals in the hope they will work together to help reveal more of the truth about how and why Caylee died. The more we can make sense of what happened, the better we can process the unimaginable horror of this story and move on. So long as the real story is not known, there can be no closure, no healing and no justice for Caylee, for our communities or for any child.

This is because truth matters. It matters in the healing process, it matters to our sense of fairness, and it matters to a little girl whose truth has not yet been told.

*   *   *

**Caylee with Her Great Grandfather Alex Plesea
the Day Before She Went Missing**

Appendix

A New and Expanded Timeline in 8 Parts

A timeline can be much like a story or narrative in its own way. This Timeline is a selected compilation of the most recognized and complete timelines available. At the end of the timeline, we provide a Figure entitled *Casey's Complex and Entangled Web*, which may strengthen your understanding of this book by illustrating the multiple dynamics at play in Casey Anthony's life.

1. Casey Before Caylee, 2003-05

- Appears to be losing her motivation to graduate from high school.
- Keeps secret from family and close friends that she is not going to graduate from high school.
- Employment records show she was working for Kodak, taking pictures of event riders at Universal Studios, from June 23, 2004 through the 2nd quarter of 2005.
- Gets pregnant with Caylee in November or December, 2004;
claims to be unsure of father's identity.
- Tells friend Kiomarie Cruz she wants to give baby up for adoption. Friend Kiomarie offers to adopt baby since she cannot have children.
Cindy Anthony disallows adoption.
- Keeps pregnancy a secret from family and many close friends.

2. Caylee's First Two Years, 2005-07

- Caylee is born August 9, 2005.
- *Cindy and George become regular caregivers* along with several of Casey's friends, including Jesse Grund and his family. The Grunds tell Casey in 2006 that she needs to make other arrangements for Caylee's childcare. Casey begins taking Caylee to a "nanny" several times a week beginning in 2006. Casey tells Jesse's father, Richard Grund, that the name of the "nanny" is Zenaida Gonzales.
- George and Cindy are reported to have frequent conflicts starting in 2005. George files for divorce and is sued by banks 3 times. He is worried about Casey's repeated lying and inappropriate behavior.
- Casey says she gets pregnant again and miscarries.
- Records from 2007 show Casey paying cell phone bills of several hundred dollars a month, although she appears to have no job.

3. Caylee's Last Months, First Half of 2008

- Casey conducts internet search for "how to make chloroform."
- Casey spends several nights a week staying overnight with Caylee at the apartments of friends. During these overnights, Casey delivers Caylee to unknown locations for unclear reasons in the middle of the night. During one such incident, she tells Ricardo Morales she brought Caylee to her mother's. It is widely reported that this is a lie. Apparently she never brought Caylee to Cindy's in the middle of the night.

- George and Cindy are increasingly worried about Casey's mysterious and inappropriate behavior.
- Casey continues to tell family and friends that she is still working for Universal Studios.
- This is the time period when Casey meets Ricardo Morales and Tony Lazzaro for the first time.
- Her friend Amy Huizenga finds that Casey has stolen several of her checks and took $600 from her bank account. Casey also stole a check from her grandmother, and stole from Cindy by using her credit cards.
- June 15, Cindy takes Caylee to see her father at nursing home. Photo taken with him and Caylee.
- June 16, 1 PM, 2 year-10 months-old Caylee Marie Anthony is last seen alive leaving the home of her grandparents, George and Cindy Anthony, with her mother Casey.
- June 16, 8 PM, Casey is seen on video at Blockbuster with boyfriend Tony Lazzaro, but no Caylee. They spend the night at his apartment watching movies.

4. Caylee Goes Missing,
June 16 to mid-July 2008

- Caylee disappears on June 16.
Casey does not report her missing for 31 days.
- Throughout the end of June and early July, Cindy repeatedly asks Casey to bring Caylee home, but Casey makes numerous excuses about Caylee being with the "nanny," and staying with her and her friends.
- June 16-18, Casey makes *hundreds* of cell phone contacts, texts and calls, mostly to Tony Lazzaro, Ricardo Morales and Amy Huizenga.
- June 17, Casey is driving a borrowed Jeep. Neighbor Brian Burner sees her car backed into the

garage at George and Cindy's home, but he doesn't see Casey or Caylee.

- June 18, Casey borrows a shovel from Brian Burner. Returns it shortly thereafter "unused."
- June 20, Casey is photographed partying at Fusion nightclub and participating in a "hard body contest."
- June 23, Casey and Tony break into a shed at the Anthony family home to borrow George's gas cans to fill her tank, which had "run empty."
- June 24, Casey gets into a fight with George about the gas cans and storms out of the house. She tells her father that Caylee is with "Zanny."
- June 25, and surrounding dates, Casey sends text messages and tells friends her car smells like a dead animal and that the smell has gotten worse over the past few days. She says her father ran over a squirrel.
- June 27, Casey abandons her car next to a dumpster in Amscot parking lot after it runs out of gas for the second Friday in a row. Her gas gauge is broken. She tells friends her car has never had such a problem in the past.
- June 30, Casey's car is taken to a tow yard.
- July 15, George and Cindy get notice to retrieve Casey's car from the tow yard. They smell a foul odor coming from the trunk that George says smells like human decomposition.
- Cindy contacts Amy Huizenga who takes her to Tony's apartment where Casey is staying.
- Cindy takes Casey home. Casey admits to her parents and Lee that Caylee has been missing for a month and that "Zanny" has kidnapped her.
- Cindy calls 911 to report Caylee missing. She tells police Casey's car smells like a "dead body."
- Amy finds that Casey stole several of her checks

and used them to take $600 from her bank
account.

5. The Investigation and
Second Half of 2008

• Starting on July 16, the Orange County Sheriff's
Office, and later the FBI, begin to investigate
Caylee's disappearance.
• Sheriff's deputies investigate Casey's claims that
Zanny lived in several different places during the
two years she cared for Caylee. The manager of
one of those places, Sawgrass Apartments, tells
police that the apartment where Zanny reportedly
lived had been empty for the four-month period
before Caylee went missing. Cindy gives police
photographs of Zanny's apartment and other
evidence about Zanny.
• Law enforcement officials learn that Casey was
not working at Universal Studios and that she had
been fired April 24, 2006. Casey admits to lying
about working at Universal Studios, but Lee
Anthony gives police copies of emails sent to Casey
from an individual purporting to assign her a job
working at an "event" there in the spring of 2008.
• Casey is arrested in mid-July and charged with
child neglect and giving false information to police.
• July 17, Jose Baez appears as Casey's lawyer.
Cindy said he "came out of nowhere" and that she
did not hire him. She tells police "she thought he
was a public defender."
• Casey is offered immunity to reveal what she
knows about others involved in Caylee's
disappearance. She refuses the immunity deal and
it expires in early September 2008.
• August 21, Casey is released on substantial bail
for a short time before being arrested for a second

time on August 30 and charged with stealing
money from Amy Huizenga.
• September 5, Casey is released from jail again.
After her release, she lives with George and Cindy.
During this time, Cindy sees Casey remove
photographs and images of Caylee from the
Anthony home.
• September 15, Casey is booked a third time on
another check fraud case and released.
• October 14, Casey faces new charges for the
fourth time, and is formally accused of murder,
aggravated manslaughter, aggravated child abuse
and neglect, and giving false information to police.
• December 11, Caylee's remains are found in
swampy woods near the Anthony home.

6. Pre-Trial 2009 - early 2011

• Early 2009, prosecutors announce they are
seeking the death penalty against Casey.
• Early 2010, Jose Baez files motion to have Casey
declared indigent. Baez subsequently receives
about $90,000 from taxpayers to represent Casey
from early 2010 through the trial in 2011. It
remains unknown who paid his fees prior to 2010.
• Media coverage increases and spreads.
• The public becomes increasingly outraged.
• Proceedings are repeatedly delayed.

7. The Seven-Week Trial, mid-2011

• Trial begins on charges of capital murder,
aggravated manslaughter, aggravated child abuse
and neglect, and giving false information to police.
• Baez claims in his opening statement that
Caylee's death was an accidental drowning and that

George helped cover-up the child's death. Evidence of drowning is never admitted at trial.
• Baez also claims in his opening statement that George and Lee sexually abused Casey. Evidence of such sexual abuse never materializes at trial.
• Casey does not testify.
• Lee testifies that Casey was warned not to call the cops about Caylee being missing.
• Jurors are sequestered and the case proceeds even during weekends and holidays.
• During seven-week trial, 400 pieces of evidence are presented and more than 90 witnesses testify over 33 days.
• Closing arguments begin on July 3rd.
• July 5, Casey is acquitted of murder and child abuse. Her parents leave the courtroom moments before the verdict is announced. Casey is found guilty only on four misdemeanor counts of giving false information to police. She receives the maximum punishment and is released on July 17.

8. Post Trial - last half of 2011

• July 17, Casey is taken by her lawyers to an unknown location.
• Casey is still involved in at least three civil lawsuits.
• Casey does not move back home with her parents.
• Jose Baez says Casey has been traumatized and needs to heal.
• July 30, Orange County Sheriff says investigation cost $293,124. State has filed motion for Casey to reimburse the state in a post-trial "costs hearing."
• Reports come out claiming that when Casey was incarcerated, she told fellow inmates she wants to have another child.

• August 1, Judge Strickland orders Casey back to Orange County, Florida to serve 1 year probation for check fraud, then recuses himself from the case.
• August 12, Judge Perry orders her to return to Florida to complete a year of probation. Baez argues that Casey served her probation while incarcerated and should not be ordered to return to Florida.
• August 9, what would have been Caylee's sixth birthday, Cindy and George attend a memorial event. Casey does not attend.
• August 10, the Florida Department of Children and Families Review of Child Death releases its final report on Caylee's death. They determine that Casey "was responsible for the verified maltreatments of Death, Threatened Harm, and Failure to Protect." Some 18 lines near the end of this report are redacted (blacked out).

References

Investigation.discovery.com/blogs/criminal=report/ca sey_anthony_full_coverage/files/casey_anthony_docu ments03.pdf. Retrieved 29 August 2011

Wikipedia.org/wiki/Timeline_of_Casey_Anthony_case, "Timeline of Events : Casey Anthony : Caylee Anthony" - 2011 Discovery Communications, LLC. Retrieved 6 July 2011

"Timeline in the Casey Anthony case" Associated Press, The Washington Post National. Retrieved 6 July 2011

Timeline from www.acandyrose.com/casey_anthony_31days.htm. Retrieved 22 August 2011

Timeline from www.justice4caylee.org. Retrieved 22 August 2011

Casey's Complex and Entangled Web

This was and is an ongoing complex case involving legal, physical, psychological, clinical, family and spiritual dimensions. The following figure is an attempt to illustrate the complex and entangled web of Casey's life.

Figure A1. Casey's Complex and Entangled Web

We can use the term *systemic* here to indicate that multiple dysfunctional systems and factors were involved.

AFTERWORD

We Can All Prevent Child Abuse and Neglect

This tragic story is an opportunity for each of us to take what we have learned from the cruel death of one little girl, and use it to help prevent child abuse and neglect in all its forms.

In the United States alone, more than a million children suffer each year, and five children die every day from abuse or neglect. Worldwide, the numbers are substantially higher.

Each year in the United States, over 300,000 children are trafficked for sex, raped and pimped for money. The average child is only thirteen years-old when she is first sold for sexual purposes, many are much younger.

Former United States Attorney General Alberto Gonzales reported to Congress that the *most common makers* of child pornography in the United States are the *victim's parents* and that the problem has become exponentially worse since the advent of the internet.

Law enforcement resources are woefully inadequate to meet the need. Prevention is critical, and each of us can play a role not only by recognizing risk factors and taking steps to intervene when we see a child at risk, but also holding our elected officials accountable, especially District Attorneys and Attorneys General. We need to mobilize to ensure that we elect prosecutors who are willing to spend ample time and resources pursuing those who victimize defenseless children and who exploit the most vulnerable among us for profit.

For starters, we can demand that all prosecutors issue annual "Child Abuse Report Cards" in which they reveal the percentage of their budgets allocated to crimes against children, and provide a breakdown of types of cases reported for prosecution, accepted or rejected for prosecution, the nature of any charges filed and the end results —including sentences imposed.

If a prosecutor refuses to release this information, we need to work together to ensure that they are not re-elected, and then fight to put into office someone who will prioritize the well-being of children.

We can also work together to monitor judicial proceedings involving crimes against children to ensure that the handling of these cases comports with true justice, and that the punishments fit the crimes.

Before we move on to help other children, let's remember where we began. A little girl named Caylee Marie Anthony was killed after being abused and neglected. Her life was short but her legacy will be long—and her story is far from over—as long as we maintain our commitment to shine a light on the truth about how and why she died. In that light will be revealed not only justice for a voiceless child, but also hope that all children might one day be raised in peace and safety.

Wendy Murphy JD,

Charles L Whitfield MD,

Barbara Whitfield RT

Atlanta, GA and Boston, MA, October 2011

INDEX

About The Authors

Wendy Murphy, JD

Wendy Murphy, JD is an adjunct professor at New England Law|Boston where she teaches a seminar on sexual violence and directs two projects under the school's Center for Law and Social Responsibility. A former Visiting Scholar at Harvard law School, Wendy is a former prosecutor who specialized in child abuse and sex crimes, and appears regularly on major network and cable news programs. She is the author of **And Justice for Some**.

Find Wendy on the Internet at:

www.PatriotLedger.com

Charles L. Whitfield, MD

Charles L. Whitfield MD is a therapist and researcher with over 30 years of experience working with patients who have had childhood trauma, addiction and PTSD.

He is the best-selling author of *Healing the Child Within*, *Memory and Abuse*, *The Power of Humility*, and others.

He has written extensively on topics including the medical mis-representation of diseases and the toxic drugs that the drug industry creates and indiscriminately sells through partially knowing clinicians to the un-knowing public at high profit.

Two companion books on these topics are *The Truth About Depression* and *The Truth About Mental Illness*, in which he describes what are erroneously labeled "Mental Illnesses" and suggests safer, proven, more effective ways to heal these frequently painful conditions.

Find Charles on the Internet at:

www.cbwhit.com
and
www.BarbaraWhitfield.com

Barbra Harris Whitfield, RT

Barbara Harris Whitfield, RT had a profound near-death experience in 1975 that turned her life into a search for answers. She became an ICU respiratory therapist which led her to write and lecture on "*The Emotional Needs of Critical Care Patients.*" Next, she became a researcher in the Department of Psychiatry at the University of Connecticut School of Medicine looking at the psychological, emotional, and spiritual aftereffects of people who have had a near-death experience. She taught at Rutgers University's Institute on Alcohol and Drug Studies calling her classes "When the 12th Step happens first."

Barbara has appeared on NPR, Oprah, Donahue, Larry King Live, CNN Medical News, Bio Channel, and more. Her story and research have appeared in Redbook, McCalls, Utne Reader, Washingtonian, etc. and featured in documentaries in France, Germany, Belgium, Italy, Canada and Japan.

She is in private practice in Atlanta, Georgia with Charles Whitfield MD doing individual and group psychotherapy for adults that were repeatedly traumatized as children. She is the author of seven books.

www.BarbaraWhitfield.com
and
Barbara-Whitfield.Blogspot.com

More Books by Our Authors

If you've ever wondered why it frequently seems that the good guys suffer and the bad guys walk, read anything you can get your hands on written by Wendy Murphy, especially this book."

—Hon. Andrew P. Napolitano, Senior Judicial Analyst, Fox News Channel

Dr. Whitfield explains in some detail how the reader can use practical and proven non-drug techniques and recovery aids to handle their psychological, emotional and behavioral symptoms.

—Peter R. Breggin,MD, psychiatrist, Author of *Medication Madness*, Ithaca, NY

www.MuseHousePress.com

More Books by Our Authors

"This book can be a great help to professionals, to people who have been abused and to the spouses of children of those who have been through the dark sea journey of abuse. There is Light here to help survivors shine!"

-Lawrence Edwards, Ph.D., LMHC, BCN Founder, Anam Cara

"Voted one of the best doctors in America, he brings his clinical experience and knowledge about traumatic memory to us. He examines, explores and clarifies this critical issue that threatens to invalidate the experience of survivors of trauma and handcuff the helping professionals who assist them as they heal."

-HCI Review

MuseHousePress.com

More Books by Our Authors

Barbara is a gifted writer with the ability to take on the complex subject of the Soul. As a Near Death Experience myself, her insight coupled with compassion, wit and humor helped me to a greater understanding of my Inner Self and how to connect with my Soul.

—Sharon Cormier
500 RYT Yoga Teacher

Coming 2012
from
Charles Whitfield MD

CPSIA information can be obtained at www.ICGtesting.com
Printed in the USA
LVOW041215081011

249685LV00002B/12/P